Introducing Economics

GW00708307

Introducing Economics

A YOUNG PERSON'S GUIDE TO ECONOMIC IDEAS

Ski Paraskos

Northcote House

For Andrew and Maria, and in memory of Tony.

First published in 1990 by Northcote House Publishers Ltd, Plymbridge House, Estover Road, Plymouth PL6 7PZ. Tel: Plymouth (0752) 705251. Fax: (0752) 777603. Telex: 45635.

British Library Cataloguing in Publication Data

Paraskos, Ski
   Introducing economics
   1. Economics
   I. Title
   330

   ISBN 0 7463 0578 8

Typeset by Nuprint Limited, 30b Station Road, Harpenden, Herts AL5 4SE.
Printed in Great Britain by BPCC Wheatons Ltd, Exeter

Contents

1

What is the Point of Economics?

IS ECONOMICS REALLY A JOKE?

The following statements are said to have been made by or about economists:

1. Economist at party: 'That's all very well in practice, but what's it like in theory?'

2. Economics teacher: 'Don't argue with me boy! We never use a simple expression when a more complicated one will do.'

3. Economist: 'Unfortunately, the evidence didn't support my theory, so I had to change it.'
   Friend: 'You changed your theory?'
   Economist: 'No, of course not, I changed the evidence.'

4. Economist to fire chief: 'Every time there's a fire we seem to find one of your appliances in the vicinity. I am bound to conclude from this that your fire engines go round starting fires.'

5. Chancellor of the Exchequer: 'Over at the Treasury we employ a dozen economists and a pair of sturdy dice. The economists advise us what to do and then we throw the dice to decide which economist's advice to follow.'

A non-scientific subject

The first of these statements highlights the weakness from which economics as a subject has always suffered. Unfortunately it tends to fall into the same category as those 'How to have sex properly' manuals, which, I'm reliably informed, you can get from mail-order companies. The problem, of course, is that everyone either can, or at least thinks he can, do it properly already. Likewise, economics often tells people how to do what they thought they already knew how to do. It deals with money and business, which most of us think we are quite familiar with already.

Compare this with a biologist. He is dealing with the workings of living organisms, which most of us do not understand. He thinks of a theory to explain something and then tests it. If the theory works he has discovered something which is probably interesting and quite possibly useful, for example that smoking increases the risk of lung cancer. His work has obvious implications for the way we actually live.

The economist on the other hand is busy talking about 'maximising your satisfaction' and 'maximising your profits'. Well, people are naturally trying to do this already; to them the economist is neither interesting nor useful. The economist reacts by theorising even more strenuously in his efforts to be as impressive as the biologist.

The second statement reflects this same academic insecurity. A cynic might say that economists use lots of long words so that no one will realise that they don't understand what they are talking about. It may be that by using technical jargon inadequate economists hope to sound more like scientists. Scientists, of course, have to use technical words because they need to discuss things that cannot be described in any other way.

The third and fourth statements, perhaps the most ridiculous, are the ultimate consequence of the economists' inferiority complex. They really do try awfully hard to be like scientists but always fail miserably. There are important reasons why economists can never be proper scientists. A quick look at these will help to explain the origin of the absurdities we saw in statements three and four.

- Firstly, there is *not always a right answer in economics*. The reverse is often true in the sciences. Take the theory in physics that all atoms have a nucleus surrounded by electrons. If this is true, it will likely be true for all atoms in all places and at all times. An example of an economic theory is that to increase the money supply will lead to inflation. However, if this is true in the USA in the 1960s it will not necessarily be true in the UK in the 1990s—or even in the USA in the 1990s. The reason is simple. In economics we are dealing with human behaviour, and human behaviour—unlike atomic behaviour—is very unpredictable. What was the correct answer in a particular place yesterday is not necessarily the correct answer here and now.

- Secondly, economists *cannot conduct controlled laboratory experiments*. They can never test the nature of the relationship between two things properly, and that in turn means that they can jump to the wrong conclusion. Consider these three graphs, all of which appear to show some kind of relationship:

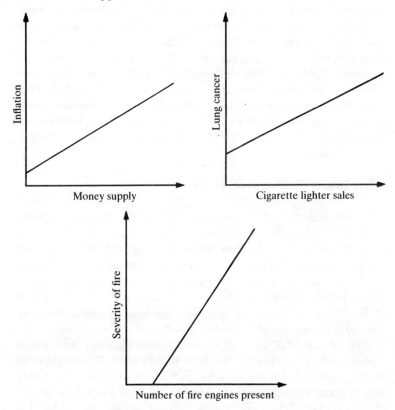

It seems reasonable to conclude from the first graph that increasing the money supply causes inflation. But if we follow that line of logic, cigarette lighters cause lung cancer and fire engines cause fires!

What has gone wrong here? The problem is that we did not test our theories in carefully controlled laboratory conditions. Because of this we failed to discover the true nature of the relationships in the graphs. Cigarette lighters themselves do not cause lung cancer; it's just that they tend to go together with the cigarettes which do cause it. Nor do fire engines cause fires, of course. It's the other way around: fires cause fire engines to appear.

When trying to use evidence in economics we can never have the same confidence in our conclusions as a scientist can have. It's not surprising that an economist should react by changing the evidence rather than his theory; the evidence is just as likely to be misleading (since it didn't come from a carefully controlled laboratory experiment). It's not surprising that economists can get causes and effects mixed up. The evidence gives them no way of distinguishing the two, as in the case of the fire engines.

And so finally to statement five. This is really an extension of the same arguments. Without conclusive scientific evidence, economists cannot easily dismiss one theory and accept another. Thus most theories continue to be believed by some economist somewhere. Economists therefore often disagree with each other and you might have to throw dice to decide which economist's point of view to believe.

WHO FINDS ECONOMICS USEFUL?

The short answer to this question is, of course, everyone. I can say that without fear of contradiction—I'm an economist! Everyone uses money and needs some understanding of how buying and selling works. We also need to know about companies and banks so that we can deal with them confidently. When you go to see your bank or building society manager, do you take an active part in the discussion or do you just nod your head in agreement from time to time and try hard to look intelligent?

Individuals who want to be comfortable dealing with larger amounts of money need to be even more aware. When spending huge quantities of it on their flat in Fulham or a Golf GTi, they may find themselves having to borrow. Do they know how to spot the best deal? When the young upward movers get older and nearer the top they may have some money to spare. What are the different forms of saving and investment and what are their relative advantages?

Beyond this, if you are an enterprising individual, you may think of starting your own business. Hundreds of thousands of British people have done just that during the 1980s. It's not quite as painful as most people think, and it has even become socially acceptable. You will need to understand not only the ins and outs of business but something about the economy as a whole. If you are to succeed you must know where your enterprise stands in relation to the rest of the commercial world.

Of course, you may not be in business for yourself; you may be working for someone else. Unless you are employed in Government services (eg teaching or nursing) you will be working in a commercial establishment. Its managers need to take account of the economic forces which surround it, if it is to succeed. To do their jobs well, they need to understand how the economy works. In the management rat race, economic knowledge may give you the edge to help you advance your career within the organisation. And it is not only the management which has a vested interest in the success of a company. The workers (whether unionised or not) usually realise that the success of their firm will also benefit them (through more pay and more jobs). The workers also need to be aware of the state of the economy to bargain successfully with their employers over pay and working conditions. Why help the company to succeed if you don't get a fair share of the cake afterwards?

Alternatively, you may just want to know what commentators mean on the news and in the papers when they argue about the state of the economy (usually, economics correspondents compete with each other to see who can fit the most jargon into a single sentence). Anyone interested in current affairs will be naturally curious about economics and an understanding of it will give you an advantage in discussions with friends and colleagues. As it is, most people launch into long diatribes about the way the world is run without much idea of what the options really are.

I suggested earlier that economics is often so much hot air, dealing with things that are already familiar; but this does not make it useless. Part of the allure of mail-order sex manuals is the sneaking suspicion that there is, perhaps, more to it than we had realised. Certainly this is so in economics. The world economy grows ever more complex because of computers and satellite communications. Our society has also changed with the new 'enterprise culture' and the move towards an integrated single European market from 1992. In future those who have not studied economics could find themselves embarrassed and handicapped by their own ignorance. Remember how it feels when you discover that the average nine year old knows more about computers than you do?

Nor is the study of economics quite as misleading as disagreements in the subject would suggest. Economic thinking is beginning to converge to some extent. Although economists cannot agree on which are the right answers, they can learn which are the wrong answers, from past mistakes. After Wall Street crashed in 1929, Governments introduced economic policies which led to a devastating world recession. During the crash of 1987 Governments took different action and recession was avoided.

The use of jargon by economists may make you think that grasping the ideas involved will be difficult. This is not so. The ideas themselves are quite straightforward, even if the jargon is sometimes not. Simple ideas can always be expressed in simple language. The object of this book is to peel away the jargon and introduce you to economics in plain English.

2

What Does Economics Cover?

BUYING AND SELLING

Buying and selling is one area of life which most of us tend to take for granted. As always when we take things for granted, we only appreciate them properly when we lose out. Without care, anyone can lose heavily in buying and selling. Companies can go bankrupt because they did not sell enough or because they sold it at the wrong price. And have you ever come home from the shops wondering whether it was really worth buying all that junk in the January sales? Were those prices really such good bargains and did you really need another pair of jeans?

Buying things

Let's begin the discussion of buying by asking ourselves about the purpose of buying. Why do we buy things? Presumably we do so because we derive some satisfaction from them. They may be things we *need*, like soap or bread; or they may be things we *like*, such as records or eating out. In either case we feel better as a result of the purchase. Economists have a jargon word for this satisfaction gained from the things we buy, they call it **utility**. We will stick with **satisfaction**. It is not just a matter of buying things haphazardly to gain satisfaction. Clearly, some things are more satisfying than others. Exactly which depends on you. If you like listening to David Bowie and hate Bros, you would obviously not 'maximise your satisfaction' if you bought a Bros record just because it was cheap. On the other hand, if you actually prefer Bros, then of course you should buy that record instead. The secret of successful buying is to arrange your purchases so that your total satisfaction (whatever it is) is maximised. This is what rational consumers do. In practice we often fail to do this; we are all prone to behaving irrationally from time to time.

Clearly a consumer will have to choose between alternative

goods when spending money. In addition to choosing which goods to buy we may also have to choose between various types or brands of a particular good. Suppose we have decided to treat ourselves to a night out, do we go to a pub or a theatre? If we decide on a pub, will it be the Red Lion or the King George? Economists call these competing alternatives **substitutes**. The number and quality of the different brands will affect our decision. If we want to travel by train we have no alternative but to take British Rail. The lack of alternative brands does not, however, mean that there are no *substitutes*. There may be no other railway companies, but there are certainly other forms of travel, such as by road or air. These substitutes for rail still leave us some choice. Clearly, the fewer alternatives there are, the more likely we are to choose the particular brand in question. Conversely, lots of alternatives would mean less likelihood of buying the brand in question.

Of course, even supposing we know which things will maximise our satisfaction we may not be able simply to go out and buy them all. After all, there is a limit to what we can afford depending on our income. In fact, it is because of the constraint imposed by our income that we have to be careful about what we buy. For example, suppose a teenager gets ten pounds per week pocket money. With ten pounds you can buy a night out, a couple of T-shirts or Queen's greatest hits. Since you obviously cannot buy all those things you must make a choice. The rational teenager (if such a thing exists) would buy whichever goods maximise his personal satisfaction. A miscalculation (eg buying a Bros record) results in less satisfaction than he could have had. If you fail to make any calculation at all and just spend your ten pounds on the first thing you see that takes your fancy, you will almost certainly fail to maximise your satisfaction. People who buy on impulse in this way usually end up seeing something else later on, which they like even more than the thing they actually bought. The result in this case is regret rather than satisfaction. If it is important for teenagers with limited pocket money to spend it sensibly then it is crucial for families on limited budgets. Most families do not have enough money to buy everything they want, even those on above average incomes. Careful planning is necessary if consumers are to get the maximum satisfaction from their limited incomes.

Buying and prices
We have so far discussed the question of what to buy in terms of satisfaction, alternative goods and income. The fourth important

factor is the price. If we find something satisfying we will buy it, assuming it is better than the alternatives and that we can afford it. However, if the price changes this will affect both the comparison with the alternatives and the question of what we can afford.

Suppose you have decided that you want an economics book. You ask around and you are wisely advised that the best one is *Introducing Economics* by Paraskos, though there are some other good books around. You check in your wallet; you have just about enough money, but there isn't much to spare. What happens if the publishers suddenly put the price up? You are less likely to buy it, for two reasons. Firstly, the comparison with alternatives looks less favourable. It might be the best book, but if it is also the most expensive it may no longer be the best value for money. Secondly, even if you are still convinced that the Paraskos masterpiece is a must for your bookshelf, you may find that you can no longer afford it. The implication of all this is that if the publishers raise the price of this volume fewer people are likely to buy it.

This is hardly a stunning conclusion. It should be fairly obvious that raising the price of an item will reduce the number of people who buy it. We have, however, uncovered what goes on beneath the surface when prices rise. If I make my product more expensive people are less *willing* to buy (because substitute brands now look more attractive). At the same time they are less *able* to buy (because their income may no longer be enough to cover the price being asked). Economists call these two effects the **substitution effect** and the **income effect** respectively. The total quantity of the product which consumers actually decide to buy at any particular price is called the **demand** for that product. As price rises, the quantity demanded tends to fall (because of the substitution and income effects). Conversely if the price falls then demand will increase. We can show this on a graph as shown on page 16.

Selling things

If we take the same approach with selling as with buying, we must ask ourselves about the purpose of selling. Why do people sell things? Clearly it is not usually because they get any satisfaction from it; going around trying to sell things to people is not actually fun. The real purpose, of course, is to gain **profit**, which presumably can be spent later to gain satisfaction. However, people's willingness to sell does not just depend on profit. They will also consider the value to them of the thing being sold. Suppose Aunt Matilda has left you an heirloom which has been in the family for hundreds of years; you may not want to part with it, even though

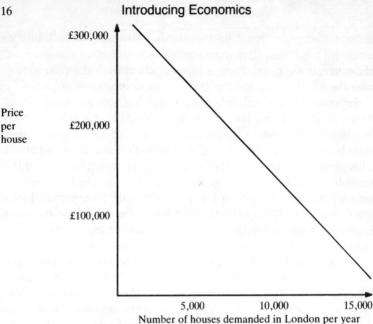

Number of houses demanded in London per year

the potential profit might be very high. Likewise, if you particularly like the house you own, then, even if house prices in your area go through the roof, you may not decide to sell.

Apart from wanting to keep things there is another reason why you might not wish to sell. To sell some things, you must first produce them and this requires effort. Suppose that someone was foolish enough to offer me £50 per hour for expert tuition in economics. Well, as it happens, I'm a lazy Greek who likes to take siestas in the afternoon and the extra work load would probably make me reject the offer. This is even more likely to happen if the product has to be manufactured (eg motor cars), since the effort needed is likely to be even greater. We can see, therefore, that people sell things to gain a material profit, usually in the form of money which they can later spend. But they may decide against a sale

- if the item to be sold means more to them than the profit from the sale, or

- if the effort needed to produce the item is too great.

An important factor here, as with buying, is the existence of alternatives. If you wanted to raise some cash and you had something else to sell you would not want to sell Aunt Matilda's heirloom. Likewise economics teachers are unlikely to sell their services as teachers if they can make lots more money with less effort by becoming stand up comics or pop stars (and if they have the necessary talent). Even if something would be profitable you won't want to do it if there is some more profitable alternative.

Even if a potential seller is willing to sell, it may not be possible to sell and make a profit. Suppose an economics teacher who is less lazy than the author decides he wants to take on some private tuition, and suppose he finds a pupil willing to pay £20 per hour. This seems fine, but what if the pupil lives in another town and the teacher is faced with a rail fare of £10? The cost of the journey in time and money means that selling the economics tuition is not after all profitable. Again, suppose that house prices in your area have risen and you decide you want to sell. If house prices in other areas are even higher, however, this sale could prove to be unprofitable, especially when you take into account the costs of solicitors' fees and removal expenses. If a product needs to be manufactured, as in the case of cars, then it may be impossible to produce and sell the product profitably. This could happen if the cost of all the bits needed to produce the item exceeds the price it sells at. Clearly, in some cases people will want to sell, but be unable to do so profitably.

Prices and selling

The effects of prices on sellers are the opposite of those on buyers. As with buyers, a change in price affects both the willingness and the ability of sellers to make a sale. Suppose that price rises substantially. If you were offered a *very* high price for Aunt Matilda's necklace, your fond memories of Aunt Matilda might suddenly fade. It would also make selling the necklace more attractive than selling something else which you might have done instead. At the same time an increase in price improves the profitability of the sale. Going back to the house example, if house prices rise sufficiently in your area then, even if houses are expensive elsewhere, it may become profitable to sell up and move. Indeed, many people began to move from south to north in the UK in the late 1980s in spite of big price rises in the north, because southern house prices had risen much more.

In short, if prices rise then people will be trying to sell more items, or more people will be trying to sell (or both). Conversely, if prices fall, people will be less inclined to sell. The total quantity of a product which people actually try to sell at a particular price is called the **supply** of that product. The relationship between price and supply is the exact opposite of that between demand and price. Again we can show this on a graph:

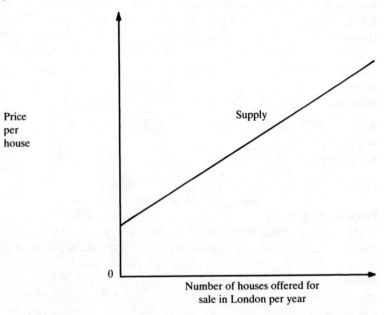

Price
per
house

Supply

0

Number of houses offered for
sale in London per year

All this raises the question, how is the price actually set in practice? On the one hand the buyers want a low price and demand less if the price is high. On the other hand the sellers want a high price and supply less if the price is low. How can this conflict be resolved? Let's look at this now.

Discussion points
1. If everybody was allowed to buy and sell whatever they wanted, what problems would arise?
2. Do sellers always have the upper hand over buyers?
3. Does advertising interfere with the consumer's choice?

HOW IS PRICE DECIDED IN PRACTICE?

In the previous section we examined the concepts of **supply** and **demand** and saw how they reacted to **price**. However, this is a curious little threesome: supply and demand both depend on price, but price itself is decided by demand and supply working together. The way demand and supply do this is by means of frustration. This may seem strange but all will be revealed.

It is normally the seller who sets the price. The right price depends on how many goods he needs to get rid of. He obviously wants to charge the highest price he can, while being able to sell all his stock. If he sets the price too high then the number of people trying to buy will be very small and he will not have enough customers. If he sets the price too low then there will be more customers than he needs and he will not have made as much money as he could have. We have established then that there are three possible outcomes when he sets his price:

- Price just right
- Price too high
- Price too low.

Let's examine them one at a time to see what happens.

Price just right
If the seller charges the right price, he will attract just enough customers to buy all the goods on offer. Say you want to sell souvenir hats to American tourists. If you have one hundred souvenir hats to sell there will be a certain price at which you will attract exactly one hundred customers. If you charge too much you will get fewer than a hundred customers, leaving you with unsold hats. If you charge too little you will get more than a hundred

The equilibrium price.

customers, which isn't very clever since you've only got a hundred hats to sell (in other words, you just end up with less profit).

The magic price where the number of customers is identical to the number of hats, is called the **equilibrium price**. Equilibrium is another way of saying that there is no tendency for change. Everything is in balance. Of course, if you find a price where there are a hundred customers for your hundred hats then everyone goes home happy. You've got rid of all your merchandise and a hundred Americans who wanted souvenir hats have got them. Everyone who tried to buy or sell at this price was successful. Since everyone is happy there is no reason for anything to change, hence 'equilibrium'.

But hang on a minute, how does anyone know what the equilibrium price actually *is*? How do we know whether we should be charging 50p per hat or 75p per hat? The answer is that we do not, unless we can read the minds of the American tourists. The chances are that we are going to guess wrong, at least to begin with. What happens then?

Price too high and price too low

Well, suppose the price we choose to start with is too high. Suppose we charge 90p per hat and only fifty Americans queue up to buy them. There we are, standing around like stuffed dummies, with the other fifty hats unsold. We could hang around all day waiting for another group of American tourists more gullible than the first. Or, we could cut the price. As soon as the price drops more people come forward to buy. This is because more of them can afford the lower price, and see the hats as good value for money. If we drop the price of our hats far enough, we will eventually get exactly one hundred customers trying to buy. This is exactly what happens in practice in the real world. If the market trader has bananas left over towards the end of the day and he wants to get rid of them, he drops the price. If you have been asking a lot for your house and nobody will buy it, you drop the price.

Now, what if the price had been too low? What if we only asked for 20p per hat? Well, we might find that, not only do we get hundreds of Americans pushing to get to the stall, but also lots of French and Germans. Suppose we've got four hundred potential customers queueing for our hundred hats, what now? Well, of course, we could let them fight it out. An amusing prospect, perhaps, but not very civilised or profitable. We could instead start raising the price. This would soon get rid of some of the excess customers. Even if we do not raise the price, some of the keenest buyers will start bidding it up by offering a price above what we asked for. Some Americans will offer to pay over the odds if we'll reserve them one of these 'neat little English soup bowls'. The price might keep rising until only a hundred customers are left still wanting to buy the hundred hats. Again this process goes on in the real world all the time. For example, if five people all want to buy a particular house, they tend to bid up the price, if necessary 'gazumping' the opposition.

Price movements

Having done our bit for the tourist industry, let's summarise the economic process at work here. In both cases, whether the price is too high or too low, it is the frustration on one side of the market which causes the price to adjust. When the price was too high, the seller could not get rid of all his stock; he was frustrated in his attempts to sell. He then reacted to this frustration by cutting his price to make sales easier. When the price was too low it was the buyers who were frustrated instead. There were too many of them and there were not enough hats to go around. They then reacted to this by bidding up the price to try to make sure they got one of the few hats available.

The end result here is fairly simple. The seller charges a price. If he's lucky (or experienced), this turns out to be the equilibrium price, the price where everyone is happy and there's no tendency to change. If he charges a price that is too high he ends up cutting the price until it gets back down to equilibrium. If he charges a price that is too low he ends up raising the price again until it gets back to equilibrium.

It therefore seems to be the case that the price will either start at the equilibrium position or will eventually get there of its own accord. In other words free markets tend to adjust automatically towards equilibrium without any interference. The process by which equilibrium is reached is called the **price mechanism**.

This may be perfectly clear to you already, but a diagram might help. Even if it doesn't, economists like drawing graphs; it makes them feel more like scientists, so turn to page 23.

In the first diagram we can see the shape of demand and supply. The quantity demanded rises when the price falls; the quantity supplied rises when the price rises. Putting these two together we can see where the equilibrium price would be. In the second series of diagrams, can you see how the price adjusts when we start off *not* at equilibrium? If we are not at equilibrium to start with there

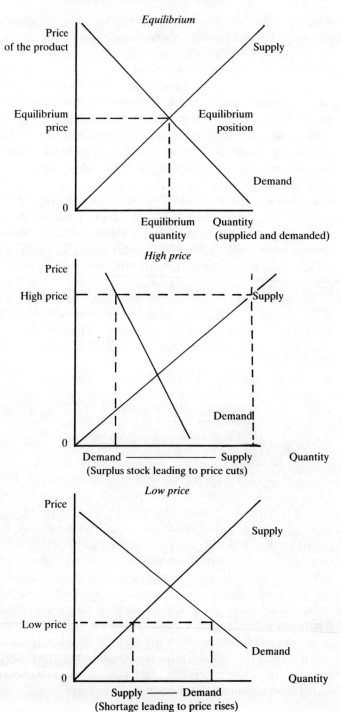

Equilibrium

Price of the product

Supply

Equilibrium price

Equilibrium position

Demand

0

Equilibrium quantity

Quantity (supplied and demanded)

High price

Price

High price

Supply

Demand

0

Demand ——————— Supply

(Surplus stock leading to price cuts)

Quantity

Low price

Price

Supply

Low price

Demand

0

Supply ——— Demand

(Shortage leading to price rises)

Quantity

is either a **surplus** or a **shortage**. In either case, the price adjusts
appropriately and equilibrium is re-established.

Shifts in the equilibrium position

Once equilibrium has been established, it may well be disrupted by
changes in the market. There might be a shift in **tastes**, for example. In the early 1980s there was a sudden interest in the Rubik
cube, a curious little device, cunningly designed to drive the average person insane. The rush of people demanding to buy Rubik
cubes meant that there were not enough cubes to go around—in
other words a shortage. We saw earlier what happens when there
is a shortage. The price of the product tends to rise. The rise in
price then moves us towards equilibrium by choking off the extra
demand. Later, when the fashion for these cubes passed, the
reverse happened. There were surplus stocks and sellers cut the
price to get rid of them. Once again, however, a new (lower)
equilibrium position was achieved.

The other main factor leading to changes in demand is change
in **income**. A rise in income tends to create more demand in most
markets except for low quality products, such as holidays to a war
zone. Conversely if income falls: as with the Rubik cube example,
an increase in demand tends to lead to a shortage and so a price
rise; a fall in demand leads to excess stocks and a price fall. All this
means that any shift in the demand position will result in a new
equilibrium through the same price mechanism that we discussed
before.

The same is true for changes in the supply side of the market. If
efficient **technology** enables the Japanese to produce lots more
electrical goods cheaply, then there will be an increase in supply.
More supply means excess stocks and prices have to be cut to sell
them off. If there is a shortage of supply, for example of wheat due
to a bad harvest caused by the infamous British weather, then the
price of wheat will rise. Supply can also be affected by changes in
costs. If the cost of raw materials such as oil rises, then producers
will be trying to sell at higher prices to cover the increased costs of
oil. Conversely if the costs of production fall, producers will be
willing to sell more cheaply, particularly if they are worried about
competition from other companies. Once again, whatever happens, an equilibrium position will be established or re-established
in the market through the price mechanism. Any temporary shortages or surplus stocks result in price adjustments, and these adjustments soon eliminate the shortages or surpluses.

Summary

We can sum up this section as follows:

- High prices lead to surpluses, which lead to price cuts to restore equilibrium.

- Low prices lead to shortages, which lead to price rises to restore equilibrium.

- If market conditions change, a shortage or surplus may emerge. But any shortage leads to price rises and any surplus leads to price cuts. Thus equilibrium is automatically re-established in the market.

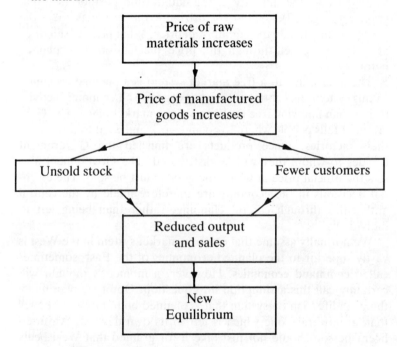

Discussion points

1. Why does the price of some goods change all the time?
2. What would happen if the Government set minimum or maximum prices by law?
3. If the Government imposes a sales tax (eg excise duty on alcohol), who ends up paying for it?

EAST VERSUS WEST

In any economic system we need to decide:

- How much to produce?
- Whom to distribute these products to?
- What price to sell them at?

We have seen how a **free market** system operates. All goods, services and resources are traded freely and exchanged at a mutually agreed price. The market reaches an equilibrium. In this equilibrium we have the answers to all three questions. How much to produce?—the quantity at the equilibrium position (see diagram on page 23). Whom to distribute the products to?—the people willing to pay the equilibrium price. What price to sell them at?—the price set through the price mechanism as explained before.

The alternative to a free market system is a **planned economy**. In this system the central authorities organise all economic activity rather than allowing free exchange in the market place. The Government tells people where to go and work and what to produce in their factories. Once products are finished the Government decides to whom they will be distributed. The Government also sets the official price at which the goods must be sold. The essential decisions in the economy are therefore made by the central authorities through careful planning, rather than being left to individuals.

We normally assume that our free market system in the West is vastly superior to the planned economies of the East, sometimes called **command economies**. However, a moment's thought will certainly call this assumption into question. Don't we plan many things in life? Isn't a system that is planned bound to work better than an arbitrary one which is left to its own devices? An intelligent person should not just take it for granted that West beats East. The case needs to be examined carefully.

The need for government activity

The idea that a totally free market without any Government interference would work at all is quite surprising. In its pure form, completely free exchange sounds like anarchy. Indeed, it would be. How would bargains and contracts agreed in trade between people be made to stick? The law of the jungle would operate and the strong would oppress the weak. Powerless people would be bullied and exploited. For a free market system to work well, the

Government must at the very least set up laws to prevent theft and breach of contract. Thus the concept of an economy without any Government interference at all seems quite unacceptable.

It is not enough, however, for a Government just to ensure law and order in trade. There are certain areas of activity where a free market would result in a situation which most of us would regard as wrong. Suppose one of the tramps at Victoria Station breaks his arm. If he walks into St Thomas' Hospital he gets his arm plastered free of charge. However, in a truly free-market system, health care like everything else would be traded for a price. They would first ask him for a fee, perhaps several hundred pounds, and then treat him only if he could pay. Since he couldn't pay, he would have to walk around in agony with a broken arm dangling from his shoulder. Likewise if a poor family took their child to a school in a totally free-market system, the school would wish to be paid. In an advanced society most of us agree that basic amenities such as schools and hospitals should be available to all, regardless of market forces such as cost and ability to pay. This principle is accepted by the vast majority of politicians right across the political spectrum.

'..and remember, if you can't find his wallet, don't bother looking for his pulse!'

Thus, even in an essentially free market economy, there will have to be a good deal of Government activity. What happens in nearly all 'free world' countries is that the Government takes over certain chunks of the economy, such as schools, hospitals, roads and defence. These parts of Western economies are planned by Western Governments in the same way that the Russians plan most of their economy. It is of course true that while the Russians plan nearly all their economy, the West plan only a part of theirs. However, you might be surprised at how big that part is. The percentage of the national economy taken over by Government activity for various countries is as follows:

UK	40%
USA	36%
France	50%
W. Germany	46%
Japan	33%
Sweden	65%
USSR	90%?

The difference between East and West is, therefore, really only one of degree. The real question is not *whether* to plan, but *how much* to plan.

The reason that passions are aroused has more to do with the differences in the *political* systems between East and West. The Eastern bloc countries were for a long time one-party states; the West has multi-party systems with free elections. However, there is no reason why a democratic country should not vote for a planned economy by electing a party which supports such a system. But this is an economics book, not a political one, so we will concentrate on the economic arguments only. We have said that the question essentially is how much planning to have in the economy. Let's consider a system which is largely free-market, with only a small amount of planning, and then compare it with a system which is largely planned with only a small amount of free market exchange.

A free market and a planned economy compared

In a largely free-market system the producers have to compete with each other in order to sell things to people. They survive by producing things which people will buy. This means that the goods and services produced in a Western economy tend to be those which people most prefer. Although some of these things may seem frivolous (eg fashionwear, eating out, pop records) they are, nevertheless, what people want. A Russian economist might argue that people do not always know what is in their own best interests. Left to their own devices they might consume drugs and alcohol, which would harm them, and do without useful services such as health and education. At the end of the day, however, one can argue that people should be free to choose. In any case, most harmful substances are illegal in Western countries, notably addictive drugs, and important services are provided by Governments (education is generally compulsory in the West). Clearly, the vast majority of things people enjoy are not harmful and there are only a few essential services that everyone should have. At best, there is an argument for making a small number of goods illegal and having Government control of a few important services like education. This does not mean that the Government should take over everything.

In a system of free exchange the price mechanism ensures that the equilibrium price is reached. The number of goods being supplied becomes the same as the number being demanded. One advantage of free markets is that they adjust themselves automatically as we saw before. But although the market is in equilibrium, this does not necessarily mean that everyone is satisfied. Suppose that there are 1,000 Porsche motor cars in the UK. With the average price of £40,000 there are about 1,000 people who decide to buy. Clearly this is equilibrium, but is it fair? There are lots of other people who would like to buy but decide not to because of the high price (me for one). The equilibrium is reached when the price has risen enough to discourage many would-be customers, leaving just enough customers to match the supply. But, of course, it is usually the poorest customers who are eliminated from the market in this process. Why should it always be the richest section of society that gets the goods?

In Russia, the Government sets prices; it sets them artificially low so that most people can afford most things. But since there is a limit to what the Soviet economy can produce, the demand exceeds the supply at these low prices. There is a shortage. There can be no adjustment in Russian prices through the price mechanism because only one official price is allowed. Selling at any other price (on the black market) is illegal and can lead to permanent residence in Siberia. The result is that the shortages persist. This is why Russian shoppers spend so long in queues. If bread has been delivered one morning you should join the queue; you never know how long it will be before the next delivery. But at least this is fair.

Allocation by queue is really allocation by lottery, and the Russians would say that this is fairer than allocation by wealth.

The Russians do have a point there. One way to counter this is to argue that people may have worked hard to earn their money and they should be allowed to consume more things as a reward. But what if they inherited their money (most wealth is inherited)? What if they were just particularly bright (a gift in itself) rather than hard working? Do people who make lots of money through quick thinking rather than hard work deserve to get more than others? This is all very debatable and conclusive arguments about something as vague as 'fairness' are always difficult. The most effective argument against the Russian system appears to me to be the incentive problem.

Suppose I tell my students that it is unfair for some of them to get a grade A in the examination just because they are clever. After all, some stupid pupils may work very hard and still only get a grade C. Instead I will give them all a grade B, whether they are clever or stupid. What would happen? I expect that neither the clever ones nor the stupid ones would do much work from then on. If hard work does not lead to any gain and laziness does not lead to any loss then why not be lazy? This is precisely the problem the Russians have had. By paying most people the same flat wage they have given them no incentive to be more productive or innovative. In the West productivity and innovation is rewarded with more profit. This is why the Gorbachev government has set about reforming the Russian system. The idea is to try to introduce incentives into the planned economy. But it is hard to see how any incentive could match the free-market incentive. In a free market you can set up your own business, which, if successful, could lead to 'loadsamoney'. The Thatcherite carrot seems inevitably to be the most attractive. Furthermore, once lots of wealth has been created, some of it can be taken in taxes and handed out to the less fortunate and the needy. If we do not have enough incentives to create wealth then, even if we are very generous in distributing it to the poor, the poor will end up with less.

One area where the Russians have, traditionally, been able to claim an advantage is in providing full employment. In a planned economy you obviously plan something for everyone to do and no one is unemployed. In a Western economy that is largely free-market we have not been able to guarantee jobs for everyone. All we can do is to pay unemployment benefit to those out of work and hope that jobs eventually turn up. Against this, there is a great deal of 'hidden unemployment' in the Russian economy, for example the use of two drivers in trains (though perhaps we have our own equivalents). Also, in a stridently free-market economy with an 'enterprise culture' such as exists in Japan, Korea (or increasingly in Thatcherite Britain), lots of people will start businesses to employ those people who do not. It may just be a matter of encouraging enough free-market enterprise. This means removing obstacles to the creation of business and then insisting that people should stand on their own two feet rather than rely on the Government.

Weighing up the evidence

The evidence on all this is not absolutely clear cut, but it does tend to confirm the view that most people are better off under a Western style economy than an Eastern bloc system. Eastern Europe is, after all, abandoning Communism. Japan has 120 million people compared to the USSR's 270 million. It also has a mere fraction of the land area and virtually no natural resources. Yet the total output of the Japanese economy exceeds the output of the entire Soviet economy (using Russian figures) by around 20%. In other words output per person in Japan is more than double what it is in the USSR. Even very poor Japanese people are better off than most Russians. However, if we compare output per person in East Germany with output per person in the UK, the comparison is more equal. There are also many non-Communist countries with relatively low living standards and extreme poverty, such as Brazil (where the country's rapidly expanding wealth is owned by a small section of the population).

I am still inclined to believe that a reasonably advanced society will fare better in the long run under a largely free-market system (remember there will always be a large chunk of the economy controlled by the Government). This may not be so in the third world, however. An extremely poor uneducated economy may require careful planning if it is ever to progress. The evidence here tends to go the other way. Cuba and China for example have made more economic advances under Communist planning than have, say, Peru or Ghana without it.

We will concentrate our studies on the Western system, especially the UK, since this is the economy we actually live in.

Discussion points

1. Why has Eastern European Communism collapsed in 1989–90?
2. Must socialism involve a planned economy?

3. Under what circumstances would socialism succeed?
4. Are there any good examples of countries where planned economies have been very successful?

3

Industry and Finance

COMPANIES

There are various types of companies with different characteristics which we shall look at presently, but they all have one thing in common: they are engaged in commercial activity. That is to say, they produce goods or services and trade these in return for payment. The idea is to **add value** to the materials acquired by the firm so that the finished product is worth more than those original materials. (It would, after all, be a bit of a waste of time if the company *reduced* the value of its raw materials during the manufacturing process.)

Four key resources: factors of production
The firm itself is made up of four types of resource:

- The **entrepreneur**, or the business person who sets up and owns the organisation.
- The **labour**, or the people who work within the business.
- The **land**, including all the mineral resources beneath it, which is owned by the company.
- The **capital**, including both the cash in hand and the equipment or buildings purchased by the company.

These four resources are called the **factors of production**. They are quite different from materials used by the company. Materials are typically of three sorts: raw materials, manufactured components and energy. The factors of production are a permanent feature of the firm. In a sense, they *are* the firm. The materials merely flow through the firm and come out as finished products. The factors of production do the work. The materials are worked upon.

In the course of working activity, value is added to the materials by the firm's factors of production. This added value should enable

33

the firm to get more money for the finished product than it cost to buy the materials with which to make the product. However, not all the value added finishes up as profit. The money made by the firm has to be distributed to the factors of production as wages to labour, rent to land and interest on capital. (Note: even if you use your own capital you have to take into account the interest you would have got by keeping it in the building society.) Only if there is any money left over after this does the firm make profits and these go to the entrepreneur, the owner of the firm. We can show all this in a diagram.

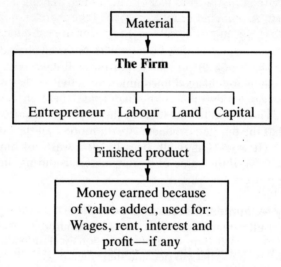

Note: Value added = Value of finished product – Cost of materials

Keeping accounts

Accounts are records of money in an organisation and are kept in books, hence the term 'cooking the books'. (I could tell you how to cook the books, but that's what accountants are paid for.) Commercial organisations keep two sorts of accounts.

- The **Balance Sheet** shows the assets and liabilities of a company at a point in time, usually the end of the year. **Assets** are things that belong to the company or which are owed to the company. **Liabilities** are things in the company that belong to or are owed to someone else.

- The **Profit and Loss Account** (see page 36) shows the income and expenditure of the company over a period of time, usually a year. **Income** is money which the company receives from whatever source; **expenditure** is the money it spends for whatever reason.

The **Balance Sheet** (see page 37) shows what the company is worth overall at one moment in time, while the Profit and Loss Account shows how the company's value is changing as it performs over a period such as a year. The profit (or loss) recorded during a year is added to the assets (or liabilities) in the Balance Sheet at the end of the year. A firm is bankrupt if people to whom it owes money demand immediate repayment and the total assets of the company are not enough to meet its liabilities. Making a loss does not in itself result in bankruptcy, provided there are enough assets (eg buildings which can be sold off) to cover the liabilities. Banks usually try to avoid making firms bankrupt. This is not because bank managers are 'nice'. Once a firm is bankrupt it is very difficult for the bank to get back any money lent to it, such as an overdraft. A bank will therefore try to keep a firm going unless it seems likely that the debts will only grow worse. If a company is declared bankrupt, the Court will appoint a receiver or liquidator who will raise as much money as he can from the firm's assets to pay back the creditors.

Sole traders

The simplest type of firm is the **sole trader**. This is a firm set up and owned by one individual, though she or he may employ workers to assist. Among other things this enables egotistical individuals who can't stand taking orders to become their own boss.

The simplicity of being a sole trader seems attractive, but there are drawbacks. First, the failure rate is very high. Second, the amount of capital is limited to what the entrepreneur already has or can persuade a bank manager to lend. Although it is easy to borrow huge sums from the bank if you are a South American dictator, it is much harder if you are Joe Public. This means that sole traders can usually only operate successfully in small scale activities, such as shopkeeping or farming, though even here, larger companies are beginning to dominate the scene. Furthermore, in the event of bankruptcy, the businessperson has **unlimited liability**. This means that all the possessions of that person (including house, car and furniture) can be taken to help settle outstanding debts. Clearly, this is a serious risk to have hanging over you.

Consolidated profit and loss account
for the year ended 31st December 1989

	1989	1988
	£m	£m
Sales	**2199.6**	2083.2
Surplus on trading (income minus expenditure)	**158.1**	137.3
Income from investments and interest receivable	**3.8**	4.2
Interest payable	**(43.9)**	(37.9)
Share of profits less losses of related companies	**14.7**	11.6
Profit on ordinary activities before taxation	**132.7**	115.2
Taxation	**58.3**	59.0
Profit on ordinary activities after taxation	**74.4**	56.2
Profit attributable to outside shareholders' interests	**11.2**	10.2
Earnings for the year	**63.2**	46.0
Dividends	**28.5**	24.2
Extraordinary items	**20.4**	19.8
Transfer to reserves	**14.3**	2.0
Earnings per share	**26.6p**	20.3p

Statement of movement on reserves

	1989	1988
At 1st January 1989	**431.0**	428.9
Transfer from profit and loss account	**14.3**	2.0
Currency variations	**(28.8)**	17.9
Net premium on share issues	**0.3**	9.0
Subsidiaries acquired and sold	**(7.8)**	(19.5)
Goodwill on related companies	**(12.5)**	-
Transfer to deferred taxation	-	(7.7)
Other movements	**0.6**	0.4
At 31st December 1989	**397.1**	431.0

A sample profit and loss account

Consolidated balance sheet
at 31st December 1989

	£m	1989 £m	£m	1988 £m
Fixed assets				
Tangible assets		**592.4**		628.1
Investments		**130.4**		144.1
		722.8		772.2
Current assets				
Stocks	**453.7**		490.8	
Debtors	**404.3**		422.1	
Cash at bank and in hand	**29.2**		36.2	
	887.2		949.1	
Creditors: amounts falling due within one year				
Short term borrowings	**(53.6)**		(166.3)	
Creditors and accruals	**(488.1)**		(503.8)	
Taxation payable	**(25.5)**		(23.5)	
Dividend payable	**(17.8)**		(15.4)	
	(585.0)		(709.0)	
Net current assets		**302.2**		240.1
Total assets less current liabilities		**1025.0**		1012.3
Creditors: amounts falling due after more than one year				
Term loans		**(236.8)**		(152.2)
Obligations under finance leases		**(33.5)**		(29.4)
Provisions for liabilities and charges		**(62.4)**		(59.2)
Net assets		**692.3**		771.5
Capital and reserves				
Called up share capital		**237.5**		237.0
Share premium account	**117.0**		116.7	
Revaluation reserve	**41.6**		57.8	
Other reserves	**34.8**		39.4	
Goodwill arising on consolidation	**-**		(67.7)	
Profit and loss account	**203.7**		284.8	
		397.1		431.0
Equity interest		**634.6**		668.0
Outside shareholders' interest in subsidiaries	**57.7**		103.5	
		692.3		771.5

A sample balance sheet

The partnership

An alternative form of company which is more often found than a sole trader is the **partnership**. Here, two or more people join forces to set up and jointly own a firm. This enables the entrepreneurs to contribute their various specialised skills to the business as well as to share the workload. For example, if I spoke Spanish and you knew how to cook sausages and chips, we could set up a high class restaurant on the Costa del Sol. In addition, more capital is likely to be available, since the combined financial assets of all the partners can be brought to bear. It is also easier for a partnership to borrow. Banks are more willing to lend because there are more houses and cars to grab in the event of bankruptcy.

The problem with partnership is that control, as well as profits, have to be shared. At the same time, the principle of unlimited liability still applies so you can lose all your possessions. Even if your partner is the shady incompetent one, *you* can still lose your shirt. This means that partnerships work best among family or friends, where mutual confidence is high (sometimes mistakenly). Of course, family or friendship groups are fairly small, so once again it is difficult to raise large amounts of capital. Because of this, partnerships are usually small companies or professional people (such as solicitors and accountants) who do not need large amounts of capital.

Cooperatives

The third type of company is the **cooperative**. There are two kinds, **producers' cooperatives** and **consumers' cooperatives**. The main feature of cooperatives is that they are set up by a group of people who do not normally profit greatly from companies. The workers are usually paid as small a wage as possible by a firm, since it wants to keep as much profit as it can. The customers are normally charged the highest price possible for the same reason. In a producers' cooperative, the workers operate their own firm, and in a consumers' cooperative the customers do so. The idea is to get a better deal than you could from those cut-throat businessmen. Each member of the cooperative society has one vote in its decisions, and the size of the shareholding by any individual is limited.

These organisations flourished in the last century and then declined under competition from large companies. They made a bit of a comeback in the 1980s. If you became unemployed and there were no jobs about, you might as well try to keep your factory going as a cooperative. In theory, a producers' cooperative should not have to make huge profits and so could afford better wages. Likewise, a consumers' cooperative could afford cheaper prices. In practice it has been difficult for cooperatives to raise all the capital they need for modernisation. They have lost out to competitor companies with access to more resources (eg Sainsburys in retailing). One must also accept that, if a company wanted to close a factory down, it was probably because it could not be operated at a profit; a group of workers who turn such a factory into a cooperative are not very likely to succeed. If experienced managers couldn't beat the Japanese, how could the workers?

Limited companies

The most successful form of company today is the **joint stock company**, commonly known as a limited company. This was widely available only after 1855. The idea is that a number of individuals, perhaps a very large number, put up the capital, each becoming a part-owner, or **shareholder**. The shares may be sold to other people at any time. Each shareholder has **limited liability**. This means that if the company goes bankrupt, you can normally only lose your shareholding. Your Porsches and Picassos are safe.

There are two kinds of limited companies; private limited companies and public limited companies. A private limited company (Co. Ltd.) cannot have more than fifty shareholders and the shares may not be offered for sale to the general public. A public limited company (plc) may have any number of shareholders and the shares may be sold to the general public.

The great advantage of the **public limited company** is that it can raise huge amounts of capital. There are three reasons for this.

- First, there can be any number of shareholders, thousands or even millions of people. This obviously means that a large amount of money can be produced.

- Secondly, the shares can be traded on the Stock Exchange (see page 67). This means that at any time if you want your money back, you can sell your shares to someone else. Knowing they can get their money back, investors are more willing to put money into the business in the first place.

- Thirdly, the limited liability principle protects the shareholders from becoming bankrupt if the company goes bankrupt. All they can lose is the money they put in, so again they are more tempted to invest in the company.

A limited company is a separate 'person' as far as the law is concerned. It is quite separate, legally speaking, from its share-holders. It can itself own assets, owe liabilities, and sue or be sued in its own right. When it goes bankrupt the shareholders do not. This also means that a businessperson who wants to turn her or his firm into a limited company must buy at least half the shares (votes) in order to maintain control. Say Lawson Enterprises is to have £100,000 capital, made up of 100,000 shares at £1 each. If all the shares are issued to the general public, then Lawson himself will have no control over the company. To control it, he needs to own 50% of it or more. He must therefore buy say 50,001 of the shares. He cannot simply give himself those shares; the shares belong to the company. A limited company is a separate 'person' and helping yourself to its shares would be theft. Ultimately, shares tend to be inherited by a large number of descendants each of whom will own much less than 50% of the company. Because of this most large companies such as ICI do not have one big share-holder in the end.

Public limited companies tend to dominate large scale manufac-turing which calls for considerable capital. Although only about 3% of all companies are limited companies, 40% of all manufac-turing output is produced by the 100 largest limited companies; they account for a similar fraction of manufacturing employment. So although there are relatively few limited companies, they are of crucial importance in the economy, especially in the manufactur-ing sector.

Nationalised industries
In modern times, especially since the second world war (1939–45), there has also been widespread nationalisation of industries. This is where the Government takes over an industry, owning and running it on behalf of the general public. The Government can do this by passing a law which forces the owners of an industry to sell it to the Government at a certain price. Alternatively, the Govern-ment can just buy shares in a company like anybody else (in this case only 51% of the shares are needed to gain control, though the Government may prefer 100% ownership). Nationalisation was particularly common in Britain and France after 1945. Industries nationalised in the UK included electricity, gas, railways, steel, aerospace and shipbuilding. At the height of nationalisation in the 1970s, these industries accounted for nearly 10% of national output and employment. The idea was to place important industries in Government hands so that they could be run for the benefit of all. A policy of **privatisation**, or selling nationalised industries back to

the private sector, has been pursued by the Thatcher Government in the 1980s. This has virtually halved the economic importance of the nationalised sector.

Discussion points
1. What problems are there if production is dominated by large privately owned firms?
2. Can large companies benefit other people besides their shareholders?
3. In which industries do British companies succeed and why?
4. What lessons can British companies learn from the Japanese?

THE IMPORTANCE OF SIZE

Firms in most industries like to grow if at all possible. Firms can grow either through internal expansion (by building more capacity) or else by merger. Merger can mean either a voluntary union of two companies or one company taking over another by buying all its shares. Apart from megalomania on the part of the management is there any real *economic* reason for this expansion? Remember that the object of the exercise is to make as much profit as possible. There are two ways ot trying to generate more profit:

- Increase the price to the final consumer.
- Reduce the cost of manufacture, so that more of the money gained can be kept as profit.

Let's consider how growth can help a company achieve these aims. If growing big is so important we will also need to explain why most firms are small rather than large.

Why managers want their firms to grow
Let's start by looking more closely at the question of managerial megalomaniacs. Why do people become managers? Well, perhaps it has something to do with high salaries. This is certainly so, but what decides the manager's salary? The answer is usually the size of the firm. The number of people working under you is usually the most important determinant of how much you get paid. There may also be a profit bonus, but the main factor is the size of the empire you control. Having a large empire, of course, brings other rewards: plush offices, company cars, expense accounts and glamorous secretaries to name but a few. One of the strongest motives for empire-building is the feeling of status and power which it brings: the simple notion of being important. The personal ambi-

tions of the managers for more material and psychological gains are often crucial. These ambitions are always driving the management on towards an expansion of their company.

Company profits and losses

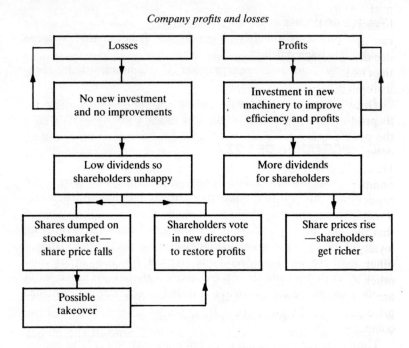

Growth and prices

We also suggested that a company would charge a higher price to its customers if it possibly could. How can a large company screw more money out of Joe Public than a small company? To improve its profitability, the firm wants to charge a higher price per item. It is not necessarily enough just to sell *more* items, because producing more items will cost the company more money. There are two main reasons why a large firm may be able to charge a higher price per item than a smaller company.

The first reason is the reputation which a large company can develop. Let's consider a large company like Barclays Bank PLC and compare it to Paraskos Finance Co Ltd, a little bank which might be set up by the author. Since Barclays branches are large and found on every high street, we normally assume that they are reliable. If they were incompetent or crooked, they wouldn't have millions of customers, would they? None of this is true for poor old Paraskos. Perhaps people who know him will be convinced of his reputation for friendly, efficient and reliable service, but he will not be *widely* known. The general public will be rather wary of giving their money to a shady looking Greek they have never heard of, who suffers from the added handicap of being an economist. Again, Barclays can advertise all of their thousands of branches with a single television commercial. One £25,000 advert can attract more people to all of their branches. If Paraskos decides on a £25,000 commercial this is likely to cost him more than he makes in a year. The large company can therefore develop its reputation more effectively.

Once a firm has established a good reputation the demand for its products is even stronger. We saw in the early chapters that if the price goes up the number of customers wishing to buy will go down. This is what restrains firms from putting up their prices. However, if you have a really good reputation and a very large number of customers, you can get away with it. So firms with reputations can charge higher prices. They may lose some customers, but many customers continue to buy because they think that the reputation is worth paying extra for. This is called **brand loyalty**. There are many examples: Rolls Royce charge more than other luxury car manufacturers, Harrods are more expensive than other department stores. Schools such as Eton and Westminster are in a similar position. Being able to sell products at a higher price per item obviously tends to improve the profitability of the company.

The second reason why a large company may be able to charge a higher price has to do with the number of companies operating in the market. Suppose that the British buy two million cars per year. If car companies make about 100,000 cars each, then there will be room for about twenty different firms in the market. If companies become bigger, and make, say 1 million cars each, then there will only be room for two firms in the market. A reduction in the number of companies is particularly likely if firms grow by merger (or if the Japanese imports are much cheaper than the British goods). In the end one very large company could completely **monopolise** the market.

In the absence of competition a monopoly can charge even higher prices, within reason (if the price is too high then people just do without). However, even if there are a few firms rather than a single monopolist, prices may still rise. A market with, say, three or four firms appears to offer the customer a reasonable degree of choice. This is not always the case, though. With just a few firms it is easy to organise a **cartel**. You've heard about them on *Dallas*; they are price fixing agreements. The firms get together (sometimes secretly) and make a deal so that none of them charges below a certain price. Several firms acting jointly as a cartel are a monopoly in all but name. It follows that companies can gain by expanding until there is only room for a few big firms in the market. If a cartel or a monopoly develops they will be able to charge higher prices. On the other hand, both monopolies and cartels are carefully controlled by the Government. Cartels are actually illegal in the UK, but companies may be able to get round this with tacit agreements which don't exist officially. We shall discuss the Government's competition policies in a later section.

Cutting costs by growing

We suggested at the beginning that if the cost per item produced can be reduced then the profit per item will be greater (assuming the price stays the same). Can a firm reduce its costs by growing larger? At first sight this seems ridiculous. Surely it costs more money to produce 100,000 cars than it does to produce 10? Of course it does, in total. However, the *average* cost per car is likely to be less as output expands. There are various reasons for this which we shall consider in a moment. To cut the cost per item as output grows is to make **economies of scale**. So, why should it cost less per car to produce a large quantity of cars than a small quantity?

The first economy of scale has to do with technology. Machinery works out cheaper for larger outputs. Suppose you spend £200 million building a car factory in Sunderland. You would have to sell an awful lot of Nissan Bluebirds to pay for that. If you made only 10 cars, the average cost per car would have been £20 million (plus labour and materials). Nissan Bluebirds are good, but would you pay £20 million for one? On the other hand, if they make 100,000 cars, then the average cost per car drops to just £2,000 (plus labour and materials) which is much more reasonable.

One of the main ways to achieve economies of scale is simply to **spread overheads** in this way. Very small companies cannot spread their overheads. They may not even be able to afford to mechanise at all. One of the reasons why Mediterranean farms are so inefficient is the small size of land holdings. Land is divided equally between all the children, instead of being given to the eldest, so after a while each farm is very small. If you only have 20 acres to harvest, there's not much point, for example, in buying an expensive combine harvester. For a start, you won't be able to afford one and anyway it doesn't make sense. The amount you save from not having to employ labourers on a small farm is not enough to cover the investment in the machine. So these small farms continue to operate in a labour intensive way which is more costly than the mechanised farming on larger holdings. In farming, as in car production, the cost per ton of produce turns out to be lower for larger outputs.

The second way to achieve economies of scale has to do with people, both managers and workers. The key to cutting labour costs in larger companies is to divide labour and **specialise** in a small firm, the workers and managers have to do all kinds of tasks. Suppose one man runs a shop by himself; he has to do all the paperwork, the loading, the sales and so on. In Sainsbury's, on the other hand, there are lots of people who specialise in different things. The managers specialise in one area only, for example, meat or groceries. They delegate routine tasks such as paperwork to secretaries, who cost less than managers. Ordinary workers can also specialise in various tasks, such as pushing masses of trolleys through the checkout queues. Each person is only concerned with a narrow range of activities and spends a lot of time on them. Therefore, each person becomes much better at their job than if they had to worry about lots of things and didn't get much experience in any of them.

If each person produces more because of specialisation, then the cost per item produced is less. If each worker produces more, then the output for each £100 of wages paid is greater; the wage cost is therefore spread over more items. In the previous section, we spread the cost of the car factory over more cars, and saw that the cost per car turned out to be cheaper. Likewise, if we spread wage costs over more output, the cost per item is less. This kind of cost saving can only be achieved when the company is large, however. A small company with just a few workers cannot afford to allocate just one task to each person.

The third way to achieve economies of scale has to do with finances. The most common is **bulk buying discounts**. We all know that you can get a discount if you buy a large amount of something. A jar of coffee that is twice the size does not cost twice as much as a smaller one. The reason is that although the sellers make less profit per teaspoon of coffee, they sell more of them, so they are quite happy about this. The same applies when large companies buy raw materials for production. A large car firm buying huge amounts of steel will obviously be able to negotiate a discounted price. This then makes the cost per car less than it would otherwise be. Large firms often get better deals from banks as well. A bank is 'selling' loans and the 'price' is the interest rate. If you 'buy' a large loan then you will get a lower interest rate than on a small one. Large companies are also regarded as safer and less likely to go bankrupt than smaller companies (they have more assets to fall back on) and this is another reason why the banks are happy to lend at lower interest. This, then, is another cost saving which a large company can enjoy.

Large firms tend to dominate the UK economy in the manufacturing sector; 150 giant companies (each with more than 5,000 workers) account for half the total manufacturing output. Large firms also account for a similar share of employment. This is far less true in service industries, of course, because services are often best carried out on a small scale (restaurants, hairdressers and plumbers, for example).

Multinational companies

A multinational company is one which produces things in more than one country. This is quite different from simply selling your products in other countries. A multinational exports the whole productive process rather than just the product itself. Multinationals can be huge; some of the largest have sales revenue which exceeds the national output of most countries. These large multinationals are commonly found in oil, chemicals, motors, electronics and aerospace. The most important place of origin of these multinationals is the USA, which accounts for 35% of all assets owned abroad. The UK is the second most important, accounting for 15% of all assets owned abroad. At the same time, 20% of the UK's manufacturing assets are owned by foreign based firms. The UK is therefore important both as a *source* of multinational activity and as a *destination* for it. Japan has become increasingly significant as a source; developing countries (eg South Korea, Taiwan, the Philippines, Brazil and Mexico) have become increasingly significant as destinations. Large British multinationals include

BP (turnover £34bn, employment 127,000)
BAT Industries (turnover £13.6bn, employment 176,000)
ICI (turnover £10bn, employment 122,000).

A large multinational has a number of advantages. To begin with, its sheer size can give it tremendous economies of scale. But it has additional advantages over other large firms.

- A multinational is not limited by the **size of the market** in its own country.

- A multinational can locate its production activities to take advantage of the **cheapest labour**.
- **Transport costs** can also be reduced by manufacturing in the country where you intend to sell, or from which you obtain your raw materials.
- Location in certain countries can also mean **tax advantages**, since some countries have lower company taxes. Another advantage is that in some countries there are tariffs (taxes on goods from abroad) and these can be avoided by producing inside the country. This explains much of the Japanese investment in the UK and other parts of Europe.

The effects on the economy of the host country in which the multinational locates are varied. The host country benefits from investment in new productive activity; it creates jobs, and helps reduce local unemployment. The host country's balance of payments benefits, because products once imported from abroad are now being produced at home. The multinational may even export some of the products from the host country. This is what happens with Japanese cars produced in the UK, for example. There may also be a valuable transfer of technology into the host country by the multinational. If the local market was being monopolised by a few large producers the multinational may increase competition. More competition usually means cheaper prices and better products for consumers. But sometimes multinationals can themselves come to monopolise the market in a host country. They may also dominate the economy in a small country, which then becomes dependent on them for a substantial part of its employment and income. This would allow the multinational company to exercise significant political control over the government of the host country. That problem is a political issue, however, and is beyond the scope of an economics book.

Small firms
So far we have done a fairly impressive job of proving that big is beautiful if you are running a company. So why are there so many small firms in the UK economy? We said earlier that large firms dominate output and employment. In manufacturing this is particularly true: small firms (fewer than 200 workers) account for only 30% of employment and 25% of output. However, numerically speaking, the vast majority of firms throughout the whole economy are small. There are around one and a half million registered businesses in the UK, and probably many more which are not registered. Of these only a few per cent have more than

200 workers. How can this be when large firms have so many advantages? There are several reasons.

To begin with, economies of scale can actually turn into *diseconomies*. If machines get *too* large and complicated they can end up as expensive liabilities. Take the American space shuttle programme, for example. Never was there a more complicated machine. The original idea seemed promising enough. By creating a re-useable craft the cost per launch could be reduced to a mere $30 million, instead of the hundreds of millions for sending up a huge rocket which could never be used again. But, as often happens with large complicated machines (*Concorde* is another example), the size and complexity lead to unforseen problems which could only be put right at mind-boggling expense. Technical delays had already pushed the cost per launch up to $80 million, when *Challenger* exploded tragically in 1986, killing the seven astronauts aboard. The re-design of the shuttle to make it safer added greatly to the cost. Meanwhile the number of planned launches was cut drastically. Now, the estimated cost per launch over the life of the shuttle programme could be as much as $500m. The European *Arianne* rocket, which is a refined single-use launch vehicle, costs just $50m per launch. There are other reasons why large projects can end up being costly, too. A big company with a massive and complicated management structure can become bureaucratic. Decision making and control become slow and ineffective. There can also be industrial relations problems. In a small company the managers usually know the workers personally and maintain friendly relations. In a large company, people feel like cogs in a machine and disruptive trade union activity is more likely. Strikes can add considerably to production costs.

Small firms can also benefit if they club together to gain some economies of scale. For example, dairy farmers are usually fairly small. They did, however, form the Milk Marketing Board. This acts on behalf of them all to finance TV commercials featuring milk. Individual milk producers could never afford this on their own, but together they are large enough to make it possible. The principle of **franchising** works in the same way. Each Kentucky Fried Chicken or Wimpy branch is owned by an individual businessperson. The company which gives out the franchises provides all the individual branches with back-up services. These services turn out to be cheap because of economies of scale (eg buying of meat in bulk).

Another reason for the success of small firms has to do with the markets in which many of them operate. Suppose that a firm makes artificial limbs. Few people in the country need artificial limbs. Short of going around chopping bits off people, there is no way of increasing the size of the market. A firm operating in this market is therefore bound to remain small. There are also cases of highly specialised sections within large markets. For example, publishing is an activity in which some very large firms operate. But there are certain specialised areas which the large firms do not have the expertise to deal with. There are several small specialist publishers, for instance one concentrating on ethnic minority interests. A large firm may not consider these specialist areas profitable enough to buy the expertise needed to deal with them. A large firm may tolerate small firms in its market even if this is not the case. We have already said that the Government tries to control monopolies and cartels. The existence of several smaller companies may help to forestall Government interference.

Other reasons for the continued existence of small firms have to do with the personality of the entrepreneurs who run them. A successful businessperson may decide to stay small rather than to risk losing control of the company by issuing extra shares to outsiders. Some people just prefer to operate as a large fish in a small pond. You may not want lots of senior managers trying to tell you how to run your company. Friendly entrepreneurs can also be better at attracting customers. Lonely old people often look for some conversation when they go out shopping. They won't get much of that in a huge supermarket where staff are not renowned for their lively banter; but if they shop at the corner store, the shopkeeper may know them personally and take the trouble to chat. Similarly, family owned restaurants often build up a clientele of regular diners who are friendly with the owners.

Perhaps the most obvious reason for the prevalence of small firms is that most firms start small. It is rare for a firm to launch into action on a large scale. During the 1980s the number of new firms registering each year has increased from about 75,000 to around 150,000. Despite a high failure rate (three quarters of new firms starting up are bust within two years) about a quarter of a million extra new firms now exist compared with ten years ago. The rush of new enterprise during the Thatcher era has tended to be concentrated in small scale services, such as restaurants, estate agents and health centres. These services do not benefit from economies of scale as much as manufacturing, so size is less important to them. They are also those areas where personal friendly service is most important, so they can succeed without being very large.

Discussion points

1. Can large multinational companies exploit underdeveloped countries?
2. Should we prevent firms from co-operating on prices or from merging into larger firms?
3. Are large firms always inevitable with modern technology?

UK INDUSTRY IN PRACTICE

The reputation of UK industry over the past few decades has been rather poor. Most people believe that British companies perform less well than foreign competitors. This is a broad generalisation and we need to look at the evidence more closely before we can come to a firm conclusion. We shall look at four different aspects of the operation of UK companies:

- aims and objectives
- location behaviour
- competitive practices
- financial success.

Aims and objectives of companies

It is widely assumed that the main objective of any business is to make profits. This may well be so for a small business run by a sole trader or a few partners. For larger enterprises, however, status and power may also become important objectives, particularly if a firm is run by managers rather than shareholders (the shareholders get the profits, the managers do not). The managers may emphasise the size or growth of the company rather than its profitability. In manufacturing, output and employment are dominated by larger firms with managers separate from the shareholders, and so size or growth may be the key motive in this sector of the economy.

However, even in a managerial enterprise bent on expansion, profit cannot be ignored. If profits are low, then dividends to shareholders will be low. Shareholders will either vote the directors off the board or sell their shares. If enough shares are dumped onto the market, the share price will fall. The company will then become an attractive takeover target because it is cheap to buy up. If the firm is taken over the senior management may well get sacked. This threat means that managers are likely to try to ensure a reasonable degree of profitability. In any case, more profits mean more funds for expansion, so that growth and profitability can go hand in hand.

Because of the need to pursue profits, firms always end up producing things which people most want to buy (hamburgers, pop records, filofaxes). If people want something badly enough they will pay a lot for it and so it is more profitable for those producing it. The most significant changes during the last decade have been in three fields:

- Extraction of oil, up 50% on 1980
- Telecommunications, up 30%
- Banking and finance, up 50% (1987 figures)

We can divide economic activity up into three main types. **Primary** industries take things straight out of the ground (agriculture, mining) and these account for about 5.5% of UK output. **Secondary** industries make things from primary products (energy supply, construction, manufacturing). Secondary industries produce about 32% of UK output (23% from manufacturing alone). **Tertiary** industries are services of various sorts and these make up the remaining 62.5% (banking and finance 15%).

The number of businesses registered in each sector is not proportionate to the value of output, however. This is because in some sectors lots of small firms persist. For example, 12% of all registered businesses are farms; another 15% are construction companies. The trend has been away from manufacturing and towards services (in 1960 the secondary sector was 40% of the economy, with 30% for manufacturing alone, while 54% was in the tertiary sector). However, this is not a very recent trend. The output of services first overtook manufacturing activity in the UK as far back as 1901. The same trend is to be found in all advanced economies. As society becomes more affluent, people already possess the important material goods and so they move onto luxuries, many of which are services (such as restaurants or foreign holidays).

Location of industry

Industry tends to locate in a particular place for one of three reasons. It may simply be a case of where the entrepreneur prefers to be. For instance he may not want to be situated anywhere which means driving home along the M25, because of the regular traffic jams (though it is rumoured that a senior official at the Department of Transport had to resign in disgrace recently, when the usual five mile bank-holiday tailback failed to materialise). On the other hand, a firm may have substantial raw material inputs into its product; it may have to locate near the source of the raw materials

It helps most businesses to be placed near their potential market.

(or a port where they can be imported) to cut transport costs. Finally, a firm may locate near its market, either to reduce the cost of transporting the final product, or simply because the product or service cannot be transported (people won't usually go very far to have a haircut: the hairdresser has to be near them).

In practice there are big regional variations in the UK, and in most other countries. These can be measured in terms of income per head, unemployment levels, quality of amenities (roads, schools, hospitals) or net migration. In general, London and the South East have the highest income per head in the UK and the lowest unemployment. There has also been significant migration from other areas into London and the South East during the 1980s, though many people in fact went back again. The average income per head in the South East is 20% higher than the national average; in Northern Ireland it is 20% lower. Wales, the West Midlands and Northern England are also a good 10% lower than average. Unemployment is twice the national average in Northern Ireland, and half as much again in the North of England. Meanwhile, unemployment in the South East is only two thirds of the national average. There has also been a tendency for people and industry to move out of city centres and into the suburbs through-out the period since the war.

Explanations for regional disparity are manyfold. One explana-tion is that some regions have tended to concentrate on agricul-ture, which has generally been less profitable than industry since the war. This is the case in many parts of Wales, for instance. Sometimes an extraction industry runs down because the minerals being extracted are exhausted. This was true of iron ore in parts of Wales and the North. Another cause is cheap competition from abroad. In the North of England, the textile industry was severely hit by far eastern imports after the war. Lancashire was heavily dependant on the textile industry and so it suffered badly. Another possibility is a sudden advance in technology. The introduction of robots in the manufacture of cars has decimated employment in the car industry in the West Midlands over the last fifteen years. Cultural factors, too, may mean a higher level of business activity in some regions: the Thatcherite enterprise culture for example is more prevalent in the South East. The shift out of the city centres reflects the need for large cheap sites and a better environment, all of which can be found in the suburbs.

Policies to try to deal with regional imbalance will be discussed later, but unless the economy as a whole is booming it does seem very difficult to boost activity in particular regions. It is so much easier to move new industry to a location when there is plenty of new industry about.

Industrial competition

How do companies compete to achieve their profit and growth objectives? They may try to improve the quality of their product or reduce its price to make it more competitive. Both of these may need increased efficiency (producing more output or using fewer inputs). Alternatively, firms may simply advertise to try to con-vince the consumers that they are better than their rivals. The tricks that advertisers can play on us are very subtle. They appeal to our hidden desire to be sexually attractive by showing how certain perfumes give men an urge to buy women flowers. They try to entertain us with commercials that have become soap operas (will the Gold Blend couple ever get off with each other?).

We saw earlier that firms can often reduce costs or increase prices, and so make more profit, simply by getting larger. Growth also fits in with managerial motives, too. Expansion becomes an important part of the competitive process. Firms will often tend to prefer expansion by merger or takeover rather than by growing internally. This is because takeover is quicker, and eliminates competition at the same time. Internal expansion on the other hand means a firm must actually sell its extra output in the face of as many competitors as before. There was a merger boom in the 1960s and early 1970s. At that time competition from abroad and the need to gain extra economies of scale were commonly given as reasons. By joining forces, firms could create economies of scale to keep costs low enough to compete with foreign companies. In fact, there was little evidence that economies of scale had improved after mergers. In the mid 1980s another merger boom began. The reason given most often this time was that many companies were being badly run and were not very profitable. Because of this, shareholders had dumped their shares on the market, making the shares cheap. Buying up the cheap companies and improving them could lead to a healthy profit. This may be a smokescreen for managerial empire-building, however.

The number of takeovers per year was higher during the 1980s than it had been in the early 1970s; the value of merger activity was much higher in the 1980s, even taking into account inflation. Mergers were running at about 2,000 per year by 1988, compared with 1,300 or so in the early 1970s. But the value of mergers in 1988 had risen to around £30bn per year. Adjusting for inflation, 1970s figures were a quarter of that. There have also been a whole series of extremely large takeover bids (one company trying to buy the shares of another by writing to each of the current shareholders and offering them an attractive price). Examples include Guinness' bid for Distillers, worth £2.3bn in 1986, and the 1989 bid by Hanson for Consolidated Goldfields worth £3.5bn.

The boom in high value mergers in the 1980s can be explained by a number of factors. The growth in the world economy in the 1980s made many firms want to expand productive capacity to meet increased demand. At the same time they had lots of profits with which to mount takeover bids. A big boom on the Stock Market also meant that there were plenty of people willing to buy shares. This made it easier for firms to finance takeovers by issuing new shares in the enlarged company. There have also been mergers in the run up to 1992. Once Europe has a single integrated large market of 320 million people, the appropriate size for companies will be larger.

The financial performance of UK industry

It is often said that UK industry has performed badly in recent decades. The British even seem to take a perverse pleasure in deriding their own products. However, to a large extent this is exaggerated. Although we did badly in the period until 1980, efficiency, profitability and growth in the UK since has been quite respectable, by both international and historical standards. During the 1980s output per person employed in the UK economy as a whole has risen by about 2.5% per year: only Japan on 3% can beat that. Output per person in manufacturing has grown by more than 5% per year in the UK and the next closest country, the US, can only claim 4%. This has meant strong profits and sustained growth in the economy. Persistent annual expansion in the economy of around 3–4% has enabled measured unemployment to fall from around 12% of the workforce to around 6% between the summer of 1986 and the summer of 1990 (more economic activity means more jobs). Many of the new jobs have been in manufacturing, which has increased its total employment for the first time in a decade. The long term trend in manufacturing employment has been dramatically downward. It fell from 48% of the workforce just after the war to 23% in 1988. This may simply reflect increased mechanisation: manufacturing lends itself easily to the introduction of new technology (unlike teaching, for instance).

This loss of manufacturing jobs, however, seems to have been greater in the UK than in other countries (except for Holland). Manufacturing is the sector of the economy in which it is easiest to improve efficiency (productivity per worker), so this is worrying. But, of course, manufacturing jobs have been lost partly because machines are replacing labour in improving productivity. So it may be that things are as they should be. Although the service sector cannot increase its output per worker very easily, the *number* of services in the economy can still expand, and so help to improve our standard of living.

A more serious problem is that, although output in manufacturing has not changed much, the **balance of trade** in manufactures has. The UK was always a net exporter of manufactures until 1983; in that year imports of manufactures exceeded exports for the first time. By the late 1980s the deficit in manufactures was around £10bn per year. On the other hand, Britain is also very good at services which can be traded internationally, especially finance, insurance and so on. The 'invisible' earnings of the City of London go a long way to cover the **trade deficit** which we would otherwise have. With the free European market after 1992 there is no reason why the UK economy should not increase its success in these fields. Until now, financial markets in other countries have often been closed to competition from Britain.

There is also strong evidence that a Japanese cavalry may come to our rescue. Most estimates suggest that 15% of UK manufacturing will be Japanese by 1995. This will turn billions of pounds of imports from Japan into billions of pounds of exports from the UK.

Discussion points
1. Is the UK an 'industrial economy'? Should it be?
2. How could we improve industrial performance?
3. Why are the Japanese investing in factories all over the UK?

MONEY AND FINANCE

Money is one of those things which we feel so familiar with that we take it entirely for granted. However, there is a lot more to 'money' than meets the eye, and a lot more to 'finance' than money. The cash in your pocket is just the tip of a financial iceberg.

Financial economics is one of the most useful areas of economics, and to many people the most interesting. After all, it's natural to dream of riches gained through cunning deals. The City has, not surprisingly, acquired a certain mystique in the minds of ordinary people. What goes on in London's square mile is not, in reality, all that mysterious, nor even particularly clever. Indeed, behind the veneer of glamour and expense accounts there is a great deal of boring paperwork and ever-present risk of redundancy. In October 1987, the stock market crashed, largely as a result of its own foolish panic. City firms have been closing offices ever since. The consequences of this can be judged by the current state of the markets for studio flats in Docklands and second-hand Porsches.

What is 'money'?
Let us begin with money. What *is* money? Essentially, money is something which can be used as a means of payment in order to trade with another party. The strangest things have been used as money in the past: salt, cigarettes, cows and wives, to name but a few. The development of money is the inevitable consequence of people's need to trade. If people did not trade they would have to make everything themselves. This would not only be inconvenient, it would also be inefficient, since people can produce more if they specialise in one thing. Trade without money can only be achieved through barter, and this is extremely tedious.

Barter involves swapping things. Suppose you want to buy this book from me and you offer to exchange a ticket to a Bros concert for it. I refuse to buy your ticket with my book on the grounds that you would have to pay me to go and see Bros. However, as it happens, I would like a shish kebab. Unfortunately, you're not in the kebab business, so you can't oblige. But perhaps Stavros at Stavros' Kebab House is interested in a Bros ticket. If he is, you can swap the ticket for a kebab and then swap the kebab for my book. But what if Stavros can't stand Bros either? Suppose he would prefer a bottle of ouzo? You will now have to find someone with a bottle of ouzo who wants a Bros ticket. Clearly, this is rather a lot of trouble to go to just to get an economics book and I expect you would have given up by now. We have, I hope demonstrated just how difficult it is to trade by barter without money. The problem of finding someone willing to accept what you are offering in exchange for what you are trying to buy is called the problem of **double coincidence of wants**. The only way around this problem is to introduce money.

Something can be used as money if it is a **commodity which everyone will always accept in exchange**. This removes the need for protracted searching to find a double coincidence of wants. The first items to be used as money were everyday things that everybody needed like grain or salt. Since everyone needed grain everyone would always accept it in exchange. In Africa and the Middle East, cows and wives were used as money. More recently soldiers in war and prison inmates have used cigarettes as a currency in the same way. The problem with using commodities like grain or cigarettes as money is that we want to consume them. Once things are eaten or smoked they cannot be used as money.

To get around this, most societies chose forms of money which did not get used up. But if they had no particular use, how would they have any value, and why would people accept them in exchange? The answer was that the commodities had a value based on being attractive and rare. Cowrie shells were used in some places, precious metals in others, gold being the most popular. Gold is 'precious', not because it is particularly useful, but because it looks beautiful and there is not much of it around (all the gold in the world would fit under the Eiffel Tower). When something is pretty and rare, people want it. It can therefore be used in exchange.

The next stage in the development of money came in the 17th century with the creation of **paper promises**. Now, you came to accept gold in exchange for a trade because you wanted the gold, but why accept a piece of paper? Well if the paper promises that you *will* be paid in gold then you will accept it in exchange (provided you actually believe the promise). This is where banks came in. They took deposits for gold for safe keeping and issued paper receipts (**notes**). If the two people trading both knew and trusted the bank, then the paper note was just as good as gold. In some ways it was actually better: for example it was easier to carry around. So although the paper promise was not a means of payment, it could still serve effectively as a medium of exchange. However, by the 20th century the expansion of trade meant that there was no longer enough gold to back up all the paper money needed.

Modern money

Because of this problem it was decided to make the paper itself money. But surely the paper was worthless? Why should people accept a paper note if it was no longer a promise to pay gold? To get around this, a new law was introduced making Bank of England notes **legal tender**. This means that the law forces you to accept these pieces of paper in settlement of a debt. The law is just as effective as the attractiveness of gold or the usefulness of grain in making people accept the items as money. So in our modern society paper notes issued by the Bank of England are the means of immediate payment, and we call this **cash**. In addition, we have other paper, or plastics, which promises to pay later, such as cheques or credit cards. Although these are promises of future payment rather than actual immediate payment, they can still serve as a medium of exchange. A promise of payment is always enough to enable an exchange to take place, provided that the promise is believed. Since we can use cheques and credit cards for trade as well as cash, they are all, effectively, 'money'.

The beauty of our modern forms of finance is the convenience of using them. Imagine taking bags of grain or gold or even cows shopping with you. What if you were using wives as currency and you wanted to buy some camels? How many camels are worth one wife? Or how many wives is a camel worth? And what about savings? How would you save up if you were using wives as money? Wouldn't they depreciate? And what if you wanted to buy something very small, like a bar of chocolate? How could you pay for it in wives: would you chop off a finger and hand it over? Our paper and plastic money gets round all these problems, and is increasingly more secure from theft than previous forms of money.

Different ways of holding money

In addition to money which is ready for immediate spending, you can also hold your assets in other forms of money. There are many ways of storing financial resources apart from keeping money in your wallet or under the mattress. The point of all the different ways of holding wealth is to enable you to spend it eventually when the need arises. The main types of financial asset apart from money are:

- Bank deposits
- Bonds
- Shares
- Unit trusts
- Life assurance and pension funds.

Bank deposits are quite familiar to most people. Money is deposited with a bank or building society in return for interest payments. In effect, you are lending your money to the bank or building society, which must pay you for the privilege. On some current accounts, banks do not pay interest but provide a service (well, that's what they call it), namely the use of chequebooks and cashcards, in return for the loan. The days of bank accounts with no interest appear to be numbered, however, because of competition from the building societies. In early 1989 all four big banks introduced interest-bearing current accounts for the first time. The banks (or building societies) use the money to make loans (or mortgages), charging higher interest than they pay to depositors so as to make a profit.

Bonds are very like bank deposits. They are loans. A company or the Government, when it wishes to borrow money, may issue an IOU to whoever is willing to lend. This IOU lasts for a set number of years, typically three, five or seven years. It carries an annual interest rate, just like a bank deposit, which the borrower pays directly to the lender. The important difference between deposits and bonds is that bonds can be traded on the Stock Exchange. Suppose you have bought a Government bond (in effect lending the Government money) and don't want to wait till the end of seven years to get your money back: you can simply sell the bond to someone else. You can thus convert your bond back into money fairly easily. Of course, with deposits there is no need to sell the deposit because you can simply take your money out of the deposit (though with some long term deposits this is not possible, and you get higher interest to compensate).

Shares are rather different from bonds. They are not a loan at all. If you buy shares in a company you are buying a *piece* of it. You are not lending but buying, so no one will pay you back. You can, however, sell the shares on the Stock Exchange to get your money out again, so you are not stuck with the shares forever. You also usually receive a share of the company's profits twice a year, depending on the size of your share. Payments of profit by a company to its shareholds are called **dividends**. Shareholders are also entitled to vote for the board of directors of the company, which means that if you own more than 50% of the shares you can control the company.

Unit trusts are funds set up to enable people to invest through 'experts' who (hopefully) know what they are doing. The idea is that you buy small pieces of the fund, known as units. The fund managers collect money from a large number of people in this way to make up a large total. They then invest the fund in a range of financial assets according to their own judgement. They will probably spread the fund across a number of different types of investment, including bonds, and a wide variety of shares. Individual units can be bought and sold, but people also benefit from unit trusts through life assurance and pensions.

Life assurance and pension funds are special forms of long term saving for particular purposes. Most life assurance policies involve a combination of insurance and investment. If you die your family receives a large payment. If you pay for a certain number of years and survive, the policy 'matures' and you receive a cash sum (though dying is generally more profitable). A pension involves making regular payments throughout your working life in return for a regular income once you retire. The managers of the funds created by life assurance premiums and pensions try to generate as much money as they can, of course. They have to be sure they can afford the payouts resulting from the life assurance and the pensions. They also have to cover the running costs of the fund. If the fund is run by a commercial company, such as an insurance company, they may also be seeking to make profits for their own shareholders. Because of this need to generate money, life assurance and pension funds are normally invested in bonds, shares and unit trusts.

Liquidity

The various forms of financial assets we have looked at get progressively harder to spend. Deposits can sometimes be spent by writing a cheque, though not all deposits are accompanied by chequebooks and not everyone accepts cheques. You may have to go to the bank and convert the deposit into cash (bank notes) first before you can spend it. Bonds and shares cannot be spent at all; they have to be converted back into cash first. These assets can be traded on the Stock Exchange to enable holders to do this. This may take up to three weeks because of the Stock Exchange account period. Life assurance and pension funds cannot be spent until a long period of time elapses, so they are much harder to spend. The ease with which a financial asset can be spent is called **liquidity**. Cash is perfectly liquid because it can be spent at once. Deposits are quite liquid; bonds and shares are less liquid. These must first be converted into cash before they can be spent. Life assurance and pensions are not at all liquid, because it might be years before they can be converted into cash and spent.

Discussion points
1. What is 'money'? Does it exist?
2. Is finance a problem for business?
3. Do we need money and finance?

BANKS AND OTHER FINANCIAL ORGANISATIONS

We have already discussed the various sorts of financial assets apart from money, such as deposits, loans, bonds and shares. These assets are all in some sense loans, and loans can be traded in a financial marketplace: loans are 'bought' and 'sold' for a 'price', which is normally some form of interest or dividend payment. Various financial institutions deal in these assets, such as banks, building societies and merchant banks. The banks are the 'shops' in which the various financial assets are traded. Let's look now at these financial markets and the institutions which deal in them.

Types of financial market
There are three main types of financial market:

- Personal finance for consumption
- Short term finance for production
- Long term finance for production.

Personal finance for consumption
The market for consumer credit finance is where people borrow money to buy something they want, such as a television or car. In other words, they want to spend money they haven't got (yet). There are various ways of financing extravagant living. The most obvious is a **bank overdraft**. You simply spend more money than

you have in your bank account and pay interest on the outstanding debt. Or, you can run up a debt on your **credit card**, again paying interest on the outstanding debt at the end of each month. You can also take out a **fixed loan**. Here, instead of having a credit limit you borrow a specified amount, eg £1,000. Instead of making repayments when you can, you pay a fixed amount each month. Interest is calculated at the beginning and built into the repayments. Fixed loans are available from both banks and finance companies; they may tie the loan to the item being bought. Banks raise money for these loans by accepting deposits from ordinary bank account holders. In effect, depositors lend money to the bank and the bank lends money to the borrower. Finance companies start with a certain amount of capital belonging to the owners of the finance company and they lend this out.

To buy a house you need a **mortgage**, unless you happen to be rich. In this case the lender (building society or bank) holds your title deeds to the house until the loan is repaid. The lenders can repossess and sell the house in the event of default. Since the sum involved is usually large, a long repayment period is needed, for example 20 years. Building societies, like banks, accept deposits and then lend them out. Since they *lend long term*, they encourage people to *deposit long term* savings in the building society by offering high interest rates. People also save long term by paying into unit trusts, pension and life assurance funds. Here they effectively save up money in a fund, which the fund managers invest to maximise returns. The savers get their money back later, for use when they are retired, or for their families if they die.

Short term finance for production
This is borrowing by companies to cover temporary expenses. To make its products, a firm will have to pay for things like raw materials and wages before it gets any money back for selling the products. Short term credit is needed to cover this cash-flow problem. Firms can get short term credit from banks in the form of a bank overdraft just as private consumers can. Or, they can make private credit arrangements with their suppliers of raw materials. These may be informal if the traders know each other well. For instance, the man who supplies the meat that goes into Stavros' donner kebabs may agree to be paid at the end of each month. Alternatively, there may be invoices or signed IOUs involved in the arrangements. In all these cases the borrowing is short term, usually no more than three months; once the finished product has been sold, the firm will have the cash to pay for its wages and raw

materials. If banks are involved, then ordinary bank account holders are providing this finance through their deposits. If private arrangements are in operation between traders, then the raw material supplier is effectively lending money to the manufacturer.

Long term finance for production
This involves borrowing for expensive fixed equipment, such as machinery or buildings. The cost of such investment, particularly for manufacturing, is huge. An oil rig, for instance, can cost £100m, a car factory £200m. Because of the sheer size of these amounts, it takes many years to repay the money. Firms borrowing in this way can take out long term fixed loans with banks or merchant banks. Alternatively, large companies can raise money by issuing long term bonds or shares (the latter are permanent and don't have to be repaid). Again it may be ordinary people who provide this finance by depositing money in their bank accounts, or by buying shares (either directly or through their unit trusts, pensions and life assurance funds). More likely, where big money is involved, City financiers and other business people will be involved. In the case of a merchant bank loan the merchant bank may have large scale deposits from big business. It can use these to make a loan or to buy shares. Or it may act as an agent and arrange a loan agreement or share purchase between business people who want to lend and those who want to borrow.

Short term finance for companies is traded in the **money markets**. Long term finance is traded in the **capital markets**. In the case of the capital markets, people lend money for years at a time (permanently in the case of shares). If the capital is in the form of a bond or shares, then these can be cashed in, or 'liquidated', on the Stock Exchange. The pieces of paper representing the bonds or shares can be bought and sold on the Stock Exchange, in effect creating a secondhand market for capital. The bonds or shares are first issued new to the original lender of the money. He can then sell the bonds or shares to someone else, so that the ownership of the capital changes hands. This is not just convenient for the original lender: the fact that the bonds or shares can be liquidated through the Stock Exchange makes people more willing to invest in them in the first place. The secondhand market therefore makes it easier for firms to raise new capital.

The price in financial markets
Having looked at financial markets, we need to consider also the question of the price in those markets. The price of a loan is the

interest payment, sometimes known as the 'cost of money'. In any market there will be an **equilibrium price** where the demand matches the supply (see page 24). We saw how a market reaches its equilibrium automatically if left to its own devices. In a financial market the same applies; there will be one rate of interest where the amount of money people are trying to lend is the same as the amount people are trying to borrow. People's desire to supply loans will also depend on how much money they have, and how much of it they want to save rather than spend. Their willingness to lend money in one financial market will also be affected by the interest rate on offer in other financial markets (for example, other banks or bonds). People's demand for loans will depend on how much they want to spend on consumption or invest in production. The cost of interest payments in alternative financial markets will again be important. People will not borrow money from the banks if building societies are offering lower interest rates, or if it works out cheaper to raise money by selling new bonds or shares.

The price of bonds
In the case of bonds, a lender gives capital to a company (or the Government) in exchange for interest. However, bonds can be traded secondhand on the Stock Exchange. The equilibrium price of these secondhand bonds will depend on the supply and demand for bonds on the Stock Exchange. The supply of bonds depends on how many were issued, and how far people want to sell their bonds. Suppose a company is in financial difficulties; there is a risk it may go bankrupt and *never* be able to repay the bond-holder. In this case people will be trying to sell their bonds, and the price will fall. The demand for bonds depends on their attractiveness. Bonds will be attractive if they pay a high interest rate, but the profitability of the company which issued the bond also matters. If the company is not profitable then there is a risk of bankruptcy, in which case the person holding the bond will never get his money back. When the Government issues bonds there is no risk of bankruptcy, which is why Government bonds are called **gilt edged** securities. Risk-free bonds are more attractive and more likely to be demanded and so there is always a strong demand for gilts.

The price of shares
With shares, investors buy a piece of a company in exchange for a dividend payout, a share of the company's profits. Shares are also actively traded secondhand on the Stock Exchange; their equilibrium price, too, depends on the supply and demand for them.

The supply of shares on the secondhand market depends on how many shares were issued and on how many people are trying to sell their shares on the Stock Exchange. If a company is not very profitable, and paying rather poor dividends, its shareholders may want to sell their shares. The demand for shares depends on people's desire to invest, and on the company's dividend payout. A profitable company usually pays more and more dividends per share and the demand for such shares on the secondhand market will rise. Speculation is also important in share markets. If people *think* a share is going to go up, they will rush to buy it; their strong demand means that the price *does* go up. If people think the price will fall, they rush to sell and the price does fall. Speculation becomes a self-fulfilling prophecy. The trick is to guess what other people's guesses will be, and get in ahead of them. It's rather like teenagers and pop music. The trick is not so much to spot a good band, but to spot one that your friends will approve of.

Financial institutions

The high street banks
Various sorts of financial institutions operate in the financial markets. Perhaps the best known are the high street banks, also known as commercial banks or **clearing banks**. They operate in the market for personal consumers' finance. They also deal in short term producers' finance. However, they tend to avoid large long term investments. The reason is that most of their depositors are ordinary people who keep money in the bank for everyday purposes, like paying household bills. Such customers put money into the bank for safe keeping; they do not expect the bank to invest it in a risky business venture and lose it. The recent fiasco of loans to South America, in which all the big banks lost heavily, shows how important it is to avoid this. Banks also provide many **services** associated with personal finance, such as chequebooks, direct debits, financial advice and queues.

Building societies
Building societies are not companies, and there are no shareholders (except for Abbey National which became a plc in 1989). The depositors are the *members* of the society and they vote for the board of management. Building societies have traditionally operated in a different kind of market. By offering high interest, the building societies try to attract *long term* savings accounts. Because most of their deposits are long term, they can lend the

money out over a long period without worrying about having to get it back. Their mortgages are typically 15, 20 or 25 years. If their customers deposited money for everyday use, as they do with banks, then long term loans for mortgages could be risky. The building society might find that customers suddenly wanted to take their money out when it had been lent to someone else for 20 years.

In spite of this, building societies have started to compete with the banks by offering chequebook accounts with interest, following a change in the law to allow them to do this. Banks are also in the mortgage business. However, it is still true to say that banks concentrate on everyday finance (chequebook accounts and personal loans), while building societies concentrate on long term savings and mortgages.

Funds and unit trusts
Other forms of savings include unit trusts, life assurance or pension funds. These are operated by various organisations. Some banks have unit trust funds, as do many insurance companies. Some unit trusts and funds are independent. Life assurance funds tend to be the domain of the insurance companies, but there are other funds offering unit trusts with life assurance cover. Big pension funds are run by trade unions, employers and the Government on behalf of workers in various industries. There are also many finance companies, whose sole purpose is to make loans out of their own resources (they do not accept deposits). These range from large organisations like Lombards, to dubious 'loan sharks', who lend money to people who can't afford to repay it, and then charge exorbitant interest under threat of grievous bodily harm.

Investment banks
Merchant banks, or investment banks, specialise in finance for producers. They offer short term credit and, unlike high street banks, are also heavily involved in long term investment finance. To provide large amounts of capital for big long term investments, they may use several different approaches. A merchant bank may lend out of money deposited with it, or in partnership with other merchant banks. It may act as an agent, putting together a lender and a borrower for a fee. Alternatively, it may help a company to issue new bonds or shares. New issues are usually only economical if very large amounts are being raised. A full page advert in a national newspaper is needed to persuade the public to buy bonds or shares, and this along with legal and other costs is very expen-

sive. The amount to be raised would have to be in the tens of millions for this to make financial sense.

The Stock Exchange
The Stock Exchange is the market place for secondhand trade in shares and bonds. Unless it agrees to **quote** a company's shares or bonds, it will be very difficult for that company to persuade people to buy the shares or bonds in the first place. People want to be able to liquidate their investments easily. A Stock Exchange quotation is also a sign of respectability, since the Stock Exchange will not quote a company without first investigating its activities. This is to prevent shady Arthur Daley types from conning money out of the public. Complying with the Stock Exchange's requirements for a full listing may be too expensive for a small company, even if it is legitimate. The rules about how the company has to be managed and keep its accounts are very detailed. To get around this, there is a section called the **unlisted securities market** (USM) where companies do not have to abide by such strict rules.

People wishing to buy shares secondhand must deal through stockbrokers. Stockbrokers are members of the Stock Exchange and only members may deal in the market. If you want to buy shares, a broker will find another broking firm which has the shares in question and buy from them. If you want to sell, your broker will find another broking firm that wants to buy.

The Bank of England
This is the Government's bank. It controls the banking system and the money supply. It manages our gold and currency reserves. It also has a few private customers from the days before it was nationalised in 1946.

Trends in financial markets
The key factor in recent trends has been improved communications. New satellite links and computers mean that financial dealers can deal with each other instantly from opposite sides of the globe. A company located in a single place can carry out much more trade in financial markets than was previously possibly, by using computers and telecommunications.

Expansion of this sort brings **economies of scale** and so big financial organisations have found it attractive. To make themselves even bigger various types of financial institution (high street banks, merchant banks, stockbrokers) have merged to form diverse financial groups which operate in lots of different markets in many countries. The large high street banks have tended to buy up a merchant bank or a stockbroker, while other merchant banks and stockbrokers merged with each other to get bigger. The result of this mixing of different types of finance is the development of 'financial supermarkets', where the public can buy all the financial services they need in one place.

Discussion points
1. Is the stock exchange useful?
2. Do we need to be protected from our financial institutions?
3. Should we all be better informed about finance, or is it better to leave it to the 'experts'?
4. Why can't everyone make a fortune by 'playing the markets'?

TRADE UNIONS

Trade unions in the UK have always aroused great passions. In the early 19th century, when unions were first emerging, there were violent clashes between strikers and the authorities. In the miners' strike of 1984–5 once again there were violent clashes between strikers and the authorities. Here we shall be looking at what trade unions are and what they do. We shall also examine their relations with other bodies, such as employers and the Government. Finally, we shall discuss changes in the position of trade unions during the 1980s.

What is a trade union?
A trade union is basically a group of workers who associate in order to improve their working conditions. There are various types. The earliest were craft unions, representing workers with similar skills, such as locomotive engine drivers, or later electrical workers. There are also unions representing workers in a particular industry, regardless of their craft, for example the National Union of Mineworkers. There are some general unions which represent all sorts of workers, such as the Transport and General Workers Union, which is the largest in the UK, with 1.4 million members. A more recent development is the growth of 'white collar' unions, representing workers with office jobs or other non-manual professions like teaching. The **Trades Union Congress** (TUC), founded in 1868, is a national body to which most unions belong. In 1988 there were 80 affiliated trade unions representing 10.6 million workers.

What do trade unions do?

You might be forgiven for thinking that the short answer is: 'They go on strike.' In reality there is more to it than that. Essentially unions undertake **collective bargaining**. That is to say, they bargain or negotiate on behalf of all their members. Since most employers face several different unions in each factory, representing different sorts of workers, collective bargaining is often complicated. Obviously the main aim of collective bargaining is to push up wage rates. Nickell and Andrews (1983) estimated that there was a 29% wage differential between unionized and non-unionized workers.

However, unions negotiate other advantages besides pay. The **closed shop** means that no one can work in a certain firm or industry unless they belong to the union. This greatly strengthens the union's hand in negotiations, because it can call *all* the workers out on strike. It also prevents non-union members from enjoying the benefits of union negotiations. **Restrictive practices** are agreements whereby key arrangements such as recruitment, manning levels or working speeds can be influenced by the union. It can control working conditions so that workers don't have to work too hard. A further consequence is that the firm may have to employ more workers than would otherwise be the case. If the union is not getting its way over pay or conditions it can take **industrial action**. This may involve an all-out strike, or a series of one-day strikes. In some industries a **work to rule** is very effective: the workers stick rigidly to the precise regulations for doing their job, and refuse to co-operate with overtime or minor tasks not included in their employment contracts. In some industries the loss of flexibility caused by this can be very damaging.

Unions' relations with other bodies

The most important bodies which unions deal with are the **employers' associations**. Employers' associations do for firms in an industry what unions do for the workers. They enable the firms to bargain collectively and set industry-wide wage rates and working conditions. If all the various companies in an industry stick together, they may be able to negotiate better terms (in other words, lower wage increases and more productivity) when negotiating with the unions. The employers have their own equivalent of the TUC, the **Confederation of British Industry** (CBI). This represents over 3,000 companies employing more than 12 million people.

The bargaining power of employers in negotiating with unions depends on the cost of a settlement as compared with the cost of the dispute. A settlement with the unions may involve agreeing to terms which are expensive (higher pay, or less work per worker leading to more workers having to be employed). On the other hand, holding out may lead to strikes which will also be damaging (lost sales and poor reputation for delivery). Likewise, the unions have to compare the cost of agreeing to less than they wanted, against the wages lost if they strike. The willingness of the two sides to settle may also be affected by outside factors. If the cost of living is rising and other workers are winning big pay rises, unions will be more insistent. If business is slack and other firms are managing to keep their prices down, a firm will not want to concede a pay claim which will push up its costs and force is to raise prices.

The two sides in industrial relations are sometimes aided by impartial referees. A **Wage Council** has three independent members and an equal number of representatives from employers and

'...and I thought they were too young to understand industrial relations!'

unions. Wage councils try to set out terms for minimum wages and conditions of employment. The Government recently reformed them so that workers under 21 are no longer protected by them. The Secretary of State for Employment can make a wage council into a Statutory Joint Industrial Council. These are similar to wage councils but without the three independent members. There is also the **Advisory, Conciliation and Arbitration Service** (ACAS), which acts as a mediator when negotiations in a dispute have broken down. It has an independent chairman and nine other members with experience in industrial relations, three nominated after consultation with the TUC and three after consultation with the CBI.

The Government itself is the other body with which unions have had to deal. In the last century, Governments took a dim view of the whole idea of trade unions and tried to stamp them out. In this century unions have promoted their own political party, the Labour Party, which went on to form several Governments. Governments of both parties have frequently clashed with the unions over pay. This is partly because the Government itself—Labour or Conservative—is a very big employer, and partly because large pay rises lead to big price rises (inflation) in the shops. The Government's overall economic policy also affects the climate in which wage bargaining takes place (the strength of consumer demand, the cost of living) and so indirectly influences the wage bargaining process.

During the Thatcher years there has been a deliberate policy to reduce the power of the unions. Four separate pieces of legislation have been passed to do this:

- the Employment Act (1980)
- the Employment Act (1982)
- the Trade Unions Act (1984)
- the Employment Act (1988).

Closed shops now have to be regularly voted back by secret ballot; workers dismissed for refusing to join a union can be financially compensated. Certain strike action is now unlawful and it can lead to proceedings against the union in the courts. The court can order the **sequestration** of the union's assets (in other words, they seize the union's money). Inter-union disputes (a strike because of an argument between two unions which does not involve employers), political strikes (strikes directed against the Government) and secondary action (strikes or picketing at other firms apart from the one in dispute) are now illegal. In addition, all strikes must first be sanctioned by a **secret ballot** to be lawful. There are also laws to ensure democracy within unions. Members of the executive committees of unions must be elected in a secret ballot every five years.

These laws were not involved in many disputes, but they did have an important effect on several key disputes, including the miners' strike of 1984–5, a strike at Austin Rover in 1984 and the dockers' strike in 1989. In each case there was an attempt to strike without first holding a secret ballot. In the miners' strike there was also secondary action, including some sympathy strikes by dockers. In the Austin Rover dispute a strike was called on a show of hands: there was so much disagreement about the result that some workers went on strike that afternoon to protest about having to go on strike!

Recent developments for trade unions

The main development in recent years has been the mass unemployment of the early 1980s. This has reduced union membership: there is not much point in belonging to a union if you are out of work. There were 13.5 million trade union members in 1979, but only 10.6 million in 1988. Another consequence has been less strike action. When there is mass unemployment you want to avoid losing your job at all costs because of the difficulty of finding another. This means that workers have been reluctant to put their jobs at risk by doing anything which might lead to firms going under. Indeed, in 1981 there were many cases of workers accepting wage cuts to keep their employers afloat.

Another important development has been the slowdown in the cost of living. Whereas shop prices in the 1970s were regularly rising by 20% a year or more, in the 1980s the cost of living usually rose by around 5% per year. This means that there is less need for big pay claims and this helps to keep the number of disputes down.

We have already mentioned the legal changes and these obviously tend to reduce the number of strikes. During the 1970s, some 10 million working days were often lost through strikes in a year. The figure varied considerably, though, and in the worst year, 1979, 29 million working days were lost (the 'winter of discontent'). During the 1980s the figure was typically around 4 million days per year, except for 1984, when the miners' strike boosted the total to 27 million. Based on working days lost per 1,000 employers, this record is worse than that of Japan, West Germany, France or the USA, but better than Ireland, Spain, Italy and Canada.

There was a tendency for strike activity to rise again in 1989.

This was partly because of the reversal of unemployment; measured unemployment fell from 3.3 million in July 1986 to only 1.6 million in December 1989. Clearly, with employment prospects looking rosier, workers are more inclined to risk a strike. Also, inflation rose significantly in 1988 and 1989 from 3% to 8% and so workers wanted higher wage settlements to compensate. There were several important strikes in the summer of 1989. A dispute on the railways ended with an 8.8% pay settlement. A strike over the abolition of the National Dock Labour Scheme (a long standing set of restrictive practices governing the working conditions of dockers) crumbled without achieving anything. This new wave of industrial disputes may turn out to be just a temporary blip, but it is too early to say for certain.

Discussion points
1. Are trade unions a useless relic of the 19th century?
2. What useful role can unions play in the 21st century?
3. Should unions be involved in politics?
4. Why are some unions signing 'no-strike deals' with new firms?
5. Should picketing and closed shop agreements be allowed?

4
The National Economy

THE-MONEY-GO-ROUND

So far we have been studying particular bits of the economy, such as markets or banks. This study is called **micro-economics**. We shall now move on to look at the economy as a whole. The study of the entire economy is called **macro-economics**. The economy as a whole can be seen as a 'money-go-round': households spend money on the products of firms, which then pay it back as incomes to households. The basic idea can be shown in a diagram:

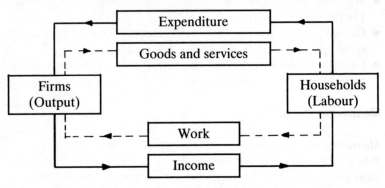

The economic money-go-round (1).

As you can see, all the money spent by households on the products of the firms must come out of the firms as income for households. Money in firms is used to pay for wages (to labour), rent (to landowners), interest (to lenders of capital), or profit (to the owners of the firms). All these people are householders, so all the money ends up back in the household sector. The only other way in which money in a firm can be disposed of (apart from embezzlement) is for buying materials and components from other firms. In that case it comes out as wages, rent, interest and profits of those *other* firms and *still* goes back to households.

Of course, the real world is a little more complex than this. For example people don't spend all their income; they save some. Apart from consumer spending, firms also spend money to invest in new productive capacity. There is also government activity, such as taxing incomes and spending money on services. Finally, some of the economy is traded with foreigners through imports and exports. We therefore need to modify our diagram like the one on page 76.

The economic system shown in this diagram is called the **circular flow of income and expenditure**. How can we measure the value of this system to get an idea of what the whole economy is actually worth? We can do this by measuring the flow of money through the economy. The total value of the money flowing through the system in one year is called the **national income**. There are various (slightly different) measurements of the national income, including the **gross domestic product** (GDP) and the **gross national product** (GNP). (Well, I did promise you some jargon.) The flow of money can be counted in three different places:

- We could add up the total value of *expenditure* at point number 1 in the diagram.
- Or, we could work out the total value of *output* of goods and services by firms in the economy at point 2.
- Finally, we could calculate the total value of *incomes* being received in the economy at point 3.

Measuring the economy

Measuring by expenditure
When measuring national income by the expenditure method, we must be careful to take into account all the different forms of expenditure. This includes consumers' expenditure on goodies in the shops and on new houses, expenditure by firms investing in productive capacity, Government expenditure, and expenditure by foreigners on British exports. It is important to count only *final* expenditure, to avoid double counting. For example, if we count the value of pop records bought by consumers, then we should *not* also count the value of the vinyl bought by the record company. Also, we must be careful to count the value of products as they would have been without interference from the Government. Suppose whisky would have sold for £5 per bottle but is sold for £10 because the Government sticks a tax on it. The 'true' value of the whisky bought in the economy is £5 per bottle, not £10. We

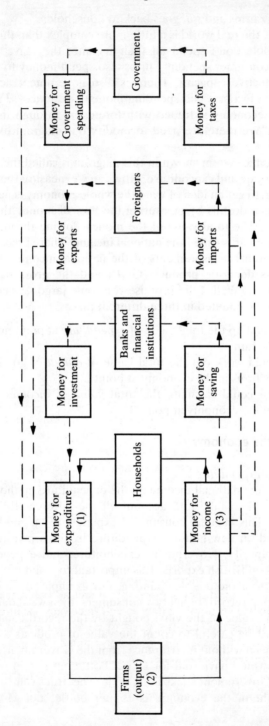

The economic money-go-round (2).

therefore need to adjust the statistics for distortions in prices caused by Government taxes.

Measuring by output

When we are measuring national income by the output method we have to cover all the different sectors of the economy, including agriculture, mining, construction, manufacturing and services. Again, we have to count only *final* output, to avoid double counting. The output of components and materials along the way for other industries should be ignored. There is a problem with collecting accurate statistics, since some self-employed people tend to understate their output for tax reasons. The expenditure method is considered more accurate; calculations by the output method have an 'error' term added to make the answer the same as for the expenditure method.

Measuring by income

With the income method, there is the same tendency for people to fiddle their tax returns. Again, an error term is designed to make the answer the same as for the expenditure method. This error term can be very large (£10bn or more) and it calls into question the validity of income statistics. Another problem is that a lot of income is not an exchange for any productive activity; it is merely a transfer from one person to another. Such transfers include unemployment benefit paid by collecting taxes from those in work and handing them over to the unemployed. Pensions are transfers between past savings and present consumption; they are not a reward for any economic activity currently going on. Transfers must be ignored, otherwise the money would be counted twice. Unemployment benefit has already been counted as the income of the people whose taxes paid for it. Pensions have already been counted as the income of people in the past which was used for the savings involved.

Who needs national statistics?

Why do we need all these statistics? Is it just an excuse for economists to pretend they are useful? In fact all kinds of people might need to use economic statistics, and since they are interested in different things the statistics need to be available in different forms. Suppose Arthur Scargill wanted to claim a 50% pay rise for the miners; he may want to point out statistics for income in other industries. Suppose you are making components for the car industry; you will want to know how much output is being produced in the car industry in order to plan ahead. If you are an advertising agency specialising in cars, you will need to know the total value of sales of cars (including imports) rather than output of cars in the UK. Because of this, statistics are needed not only in various forms but also in great detail. The Government's Central Statistical Office publishes a **Blue Book** full of such details.

The most interesting statistics, however, are not the detailed breakdowns but the overall totals for national income. We need these to make both historical and geographical comparisons. We always want to know if we are better off than we were a few years ago, and we are obsessed with whether we are better off than the Americans, Germans, Japanese or French (we aren't). The GNP of the UK for 1988 was £370 billion. There are, however, a number of problems we need to think about when making historical and geographical comparisons using national income statistics.

Problems of using statistics

Comparing past and present
For historical comparisons, the main problem is that prices tend to rise over time (inflation). For example, a look at the national income for 1960 may show that, by 1990, the national income was twenty times greater than it had been. But, of course, this does not mean that there is twenty times as much economic activity, nor that we are twenty times better off. In reality, most things are, on average, ten times as expensive, so that we are only twice as well off. It is possible to make statistical adjustments to take price changes into account. Figures for 1990 can be produced in 1960 prices, or figures for 1960 can be produced in 1990 prices.

Another problem with comparing the value of the economy over time is that the *quality* of products changes. For instance, a £200 television in 1960 is quite pathetic compared to a £200 television in 1990, which will have colour, better definition and remote control. Changes in quality simply cannot be accounted for in statistics, because statistics only measure *quantity*.

Comparing different countries
Problems in making geographical comparisons are more numerous. The first is population. Suppose China and Spain have the same national income. Does this mean that a Chinaman and a Spaniard are equally well off? Clearly not—there are only 40 million Spaniards but 1,000 million Chinese. We can get around this by calculating national income *per head* of population (divid-

ing national income by the number of people). This gives us income per person, or **income per capita**, which enables us to compare living standards. But even income per person is misleading if there are differences in how income is distributed. For instance, the income per head in Brazil is almost as high as it is in Portugal (which is appropriate, since the Portugese ran the place for hundreds of years). However, income in Brazil is extremely uneven. There are a few super-rich business people, but the vast majority of Brazilians live in shanty towns made of corrugated iron and cardboard, without any proper sanitation or amenities. This is not true in Portugal, where the distribution of income is far more even and most poor people have a passable standard of living.

Another problem in comparing different countries is that the composition of output varies. For instance, the USSR has a total national income almost as big as that of Japan. However, as much as 20% of the USSR's goes in military expenditure, whereas in Japan the figure is only 1%. We also need to remember that the material standard of living is not the same thing as the quality of life. Although the average Greek is only half as rich as the average English person, Greeks spend far more time relaxing. Greeks like me are lazy; they take siestas in the afternoon and spend long pleasant hours down at the taverna. Even if the Greek standard of living is half that in England, the Greek quality of life may not be.

Further problems with statistics arise when we take into account natural resources. Although Ethiopia finds it difficult to produce anything very much, this is not necessarily the fault of the Ethiopians: they have hardly any water, their soil is infertile and there are no large deposits of minerals. On the other hand, the Japanese do very well, even though they have no natural resources either.

Another complication is that in some countries there is a great deal of self-help, such as growing your own food or DIY home improvements. Since no expenditure or income is involved, these activities are not measured in the national income accounts. Other activities not counted in the statistics include trade in illegal substances (drugs and prostitution) and illegal jobs (done by people who are also claiming unemployment benefit). Such illegal activities are nicknamed the **black economy**. It has been estimated that 25% of Italian output is in the black economy, compared with about 7% in the UK. This means that the official national income accounts for Italy are very misleading.

Other statistical problems
Finally there are various purely technical problems. In order to

compare different countries, we have to use the same currency, but of course countries have different currencies. Suppose the average British person earns £12,000 per year, while the average French person earns F120,000. Since you can exchange £1 for F10, this seems to show that the standard of living is about the same. But the exchange rate varies for all sorts of reasons to do with trade and speculation in the money markets. £1 may not actually buy the same things in Britain that F10 buy in France. A better comparison can be made by working out the purchasing power of the two currencies, and then calculating an exchange rate from this. There are other statistical problems, however, which cannot be dealt with so easily. Different countries calculate their national income statistics in different ways. This problem makes strict comparisons invalid.

Discussion points
1. How many times do you think money goes round the circular flow of income and expenditure in one year?
2. What decides the level of economic activity in a country?
3. Why are some countries so poor?

ADJUSTMENTS IN THE ECONOMY

We discussed earlier the circular flow of income and expenditure in the economy as a whole. This system will be in equilibrium (in other words, not changing) when it is balanced. There are two aspects to this balance:

- The total amount of money being supplied into the system must be the same as the total demand for money in the system.
- The total attempts at expenditure in the system must be the same as the total amount of income in the system.

If either of these two balances is disturbed, the system will be in disequilibrium (tending to change). We then need to consider how it behaves and whether it adjusts back to equilibrium.

Money and the economy: Keynesians and monetarists
Let us begin by looking at the balance of money in the economy. If the supply of money is equal to the demand for money, then the system is in equilibrium. If the supply of money is more, or less, than the demand for money the system is imbalanced. How the economy adjusts to this imbalance is the subject of much disagreement between economists (but then, what isn't?). There are two

main schools of thought, the **Keynesians** and the **monetarists**. They disagree fundamentally about what money is used for; this lies at the heart of their disagreements on most other issues.

The Keynesians

The Keynesians are followers of John Maynard Keynes, a Cambridge economist of the 1930s. They believe that money is held in cash or liquid form for two very different purposes. The first is for spending on regular transactions (including some for emergencies). You keep a certain amount each week for family groceries (and some spare in case you accidentally break the best crockery while washing up). The second is for speculative investment (holding money in case a good share offer or business opportunity comes up). If there is an imbalance in the money markets, then either the money supply is greater than the demand for money, or the other way around.

Suppose the Government prints more money, or the banks make more credit available for example by issuing lots of credit cards. The money supply will rise above the current demand for money. When there is an excessive supply of something, its price is reduced to clear stocks. The price of money is the interest rate on loans. With cheaper interest rates, people tend to take out more loans—in effect, demanding more money. The extra money will partly be spent on extra consumption, but partly also on extra investment in business activities. So, while consumption rises, production rises too. This means that it might be possible to produce more goods and services to meet the extra expenditure in the shops by consumers. If firms cannot produce enough extra goods to meet the extra expenditure, they may put up their prices instead (people have more money to spend, so they will pay higher prices).

The other type of imbalance occurs when people are keen to get money for consumer spending, or for business investment, or both. If the demand for money exceeds the supply, then, as in any market, the price will rise. The price of money is the interest rate on loans. Because of the higher interest rate, more credit may be made available so that the extra demand for money can be satisfied. As the interest rate rises, however, the extra demand for credit will tend to be discouraged. Probably some extra credit will get into the system and there will be more money around. Regardless of whether it is the supply or the demand for money which rises, in the end, we end up with more money flowing round the system. The effects will be the same as before: more spending and

possibly more investment. There will be more consumption, and
perhaps more production, and again there may be price rises.

The monetarists
The monetarists, under the influence of Professor Milton Fried-
man of Chicago in the 1960s, originally believed that people hold
money in cash or liquid form for one purpose only—to spend it on
consumption. When they make financial plans, finance for savings
and investment is kept quite separate from money for spending.
Savings are not held in liquid form, but in long term savings
accounts, bonds or shares. Since they are planned and organised
separately, money for spending does not affect finance for saving. If
there is any extra cash available, people will blow it on something
frivolous (a satellite TV dish for instance). Therefore, extra cash will
only affect spending on consumption, not savings for investment.

   If the money in circulation rises, for whatever reason, the
effects are different from what the Keynesians predict. In the
monetarist system, the extra cash in your pocket is all spent on
extra consumption. None of it goes on extra investment in new
business activity. Because of this, there is no extra productive
capacity in firms to meet the extra spending by consumers. They
can only react by putting up their prices. If people are trying to
spend more money but cannot spend it on more goods, they can
only spend it by paying higher prices. People have more money so
they are willing to pay higher prices.

   This disagreement about what money is for and how it is used
leads to different predictions about what will happen in the economy if more money is introduced into the circular flow system. We
could, of course, test this by looking to see whether extra money is
spent just on consumption or whether some of it goes into investment. The statistical evidence, which is always hotly contested by
economists, does seem to show some interplay between money for
spending and finance for saving and investment. The question of
degree is still open to doubt, however, and there are in any case
other disagreements between Keynesians and monetarists. Whichever you believe, once extra money is created it moves around the
circular flow system. The amount of money being spent by households on the products of firms rises. Firms then pay more money
back to households as income and they have more to spend, and so
on. The only dispute is about whether this extra money represents
spending on extra output, or spending at higher prices. The flow-
chart on page 83 shows this difference between the two schools of
thought.

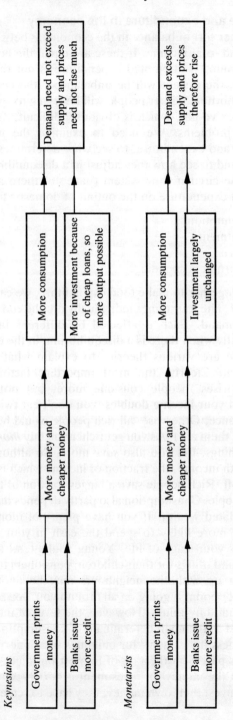

Keynesians

| Government prints money | → | More money and cheaper money | → | More consumption | → | Demand need not exceed supply and prices need not rise much |
| Banks issue more credit | → | More money and cheaper money | → | More investment because of cheap loans, so more output possible | |

Monetarists

| Government prints money | → | More money and cheaper money | → | More consumption | → | Demand exceeds supply and prices therefore rise |
| Banks issue more credit | → | More money and cheaper money | → | Investment largely unchanged | |

Income and expenditure in the economy

The other sort of balance in the economy is between total expenditure and total income. If these are equal the economy will be in equilibrium. If attempted expenditure is not the same as actual income, the system will be unbalanced: the economy will be in disequilibrium. Either people will be trying to spend more money than they've got, which is obviously difficult, or less, which also causes problems. We need to examine the make-up of both income and expenditure, to see what determines them in the first place, and to see how they adjust in a disequilibrium situation.

In the circular flow system (page 76) there are four different types of expenditure on the output of domestic firms:

- consumption
- investment
- exports
- Government spending.

Taken together to make total expenditure, we call them **aggregate demand**. The four things individually are the **components of aggregate demand**. Each is affected by different factors and reacts differently when there is a disequilibrium in the economy.

There are various theories to explain what determines consumption. Clearly, the most important factor is income. As income rises, people consume more, but not proportionately more. If your income doubles, you don't eat twice as much food, for instance. Otherwise, all rich people would be blobs (and only some of them are). As you get richer you buy *more* things, you buy *better* things, but you also *save* more. So although consumption rises with income, the fraction of income which is consumed tends to fall off. Rich people save a bigger fraction of their income than poor people. Consumption also partly depends on the state of your accumulated wealth. If you have plenty of money stashed away you are more likely to spend the cash in your pocket. Another factor is your stage of life. Young adults tend to spend a lot on houses and things for their children; pensioners tend to spend less. Keeping up with the neighbours may be another factor. If a consumer boom is going on all around you, you are more likely to go out and buy things. However, the level of income is generally regarded as the main determinant of consumption.

Business investment, for buildings, machinery and equipment, depends partly on the rate of interest on loans. Why?—because much of the money for investment is borrowed. Even when companies invest their own money, they have to remember the interest they *would* have received from putting it into a bank deposit. However, business investment also depends on the expected gains in profitability arising from the investment. The profits gained will depend on how many customers are willing to buy the output from the investment, and how much they are willing to pay for it. This will be affected by the general level of incomes in the economy. The higher the total national income, the more money people will have to spend, so they are likely to be willing to buy more products at a higher price. This makes investment in productive capacity more promising, and so is more likely to happen when incomes are high and rising.

Government spending depends on all sorts of factors, both political and economic. The total level and directions of Government spending depend on the political complexion of the Government. For example, Labour Governments generally want to spend more money, as a fraction of the economy, than Conservative ones, and more of it on social projects and less on defence. The economic policy of the Government of the day will also be important. If there is too much consumption in the economy, then the Government may cut back its own spending to try to restore balance to the system. On the other hand, if a General Election is coming up, spending on all sorts of services is likely to increase, and taxes may well be reduced to buy votes.

Exports depend heavily on the incomes and tastes of the foreigners who buy them. However, we can improve the prospects of selling exports to foreigners through our own efforts. We can't live on past glories: we have to produce things which the world actually wants to buy, made to a high quality, and offered for sale at a competitive price. Efficient production and effective marketing are the keys to success. The domestic economy can affect exports as well, though. If there is very strong demand for products by domestic consumers, then firms will be tempted to sell products at home, which is usually easier. In this case, there may not be as much production available for attempts at export sales.

Incomes in the economy are allocated in a number of different ways. Firstly, a good deal of income disappears in taxation, taken by the Government to finance its spending. Of the rest, some is saved. Saving may either be an active decision (some people have specific savings targets) or it may be passive (some savings is just what is left over from consumption). Of that which is spent on consumption, some is spent on imports of foreign goods, because they are better, or cheaper, or just different from British goods.

Only money spent on domestic consumption is bound to con-

tinue on its way around the circular flow of income and expenditure. Money taken out in taxes need not be spent later on. The
Government can spend less than it takes in taxes or it can spend
more (by printing it or borrowing it). Money being saved in banks
or building societies need not be borrowed by business for investment later. Business people may borrow less than all the savings
available, or more (by borrowing from abroad, for instance).
Money spent buying goods from foreigners need not be spent by
foreigners buying goods from us. Foreigners can spend either
more or less in the UK than we do abroad. As you can see, there is
great scope for imbalance in the economy since the total income
earned will not necessarily all be spent.

If total expenditure, including all the various components of
aggregate demand, exceeds total income, then extra money (cash
or credit) will be needed to finance the extra expenditure. If the
Government allows the extra money into the system, then the
level of total expenditure can rise. If some people are spending
more money, then other people will be earning more—so they will
spend more money and the rate of economic activity speeds up.
This is called the **multiplier** process. The effects of this will be
different according to whether you are a Keynesian or a monetarist:

- The **Keynesians** think that some of the extra expenditure will go
  on consumption, and some on extra production. There may be
  some extra output and some rise in prices.
- The **monetarists** think that investment in extra output is
  unlikely: firms will react to the extra consumption by putting up
  their prices.

Either way, once extra money is being spent in the circular flow
system, it will come out as extra income to households. The extra
income is then spent again, so that the amount of money flowing
around the system is greater. Again, the dispute is over whether
the extra money is spent on extra output or whether it is spent on
higher prices.

Summary
When the amount of money flowing around the circular flow
system increases, the value of the economy appears greater. In
other words, when we measure the economic activity in money
terms (see page 75) we get a bigger answer. From what we have
been saying, increases in activity can be caused either by introducing more money into the circular flow system, or by an increase in

desired spending. But even if people want to spend more, they can only do so if the Government allows cash or credit to expand; so more money is still the key. The reverse of this also follows. A drop in economic activity can be caused either by taking money out of circulation or by a decrease in desired spending. To control the economy, a Government must, therefore, maintain control of the supply of money (both cash and credit). This is now widely accepted by most economists.

Discussion points
1. Who are most likely to be correct in their view of money, Keynesians or monetarists?
2. Why can't we conduct an experiment to get a conclusive answer?

IMPROVEMENTS IN LIVING STANDARDS

Living standards improve when the value of goods and services available to each person increases. This means an increase in the quality, or quantity, of output of goods and services, assuming the population does not change. An increase in the total output of goods and services (measured by money value) in the economy is what we call **growth**.

How can we get growth? To get more output, we could stimulate more demand by consumers: if consumers spend more, firms are likely to produce more. Alternatively, we could improve the inputs of resources which go into products so that we can increase the output of goods and services. Early on, we identified five types of resources. These were materials used in production and the four factors of production (land, capital, labour and enterprise) which go to make up a firm and which do the work. In practice, of course, raw materials always come out of the land; we can thus classify materials and land together as 'natural resources'. If we can increase the quantity or quality of any or all of these resources which go into production, we should be able to get more out of production.

How can we improve living standards?

More consumption
If people buy more products, firms may be tempted to produce more. To make this happen we will have to persuade people to save less, or put more money into their pockets. If the economy

seems to be going well and jobs are secure, families may choose to save less and spend more. This seems to be what happened in 1988, for instance. People can have more money in their pockets if the Government cuts taxes (as it did in 1988) or if credit is easier to get hold of (1988 again). Even if firms don't respond by producing more, the extra spending goes instead on goods imported from abroad. Either way people end up consuming more. The effect is higher living standards.

More natural resources
The simplest way of improving living standards is to get more natural resources into the economy. Increasing the quantity or quality of land is difficult, but it can be done. Land can be cleared or drained or accessed; it can even be reclaimed from the sea (as in the case of the Dutch polders). The availability of mineral deposits or energy reserves depends on exploration. The discovery of North Sea oil is an example. The total output possible in the UK economy increased by about 7% as a result of the North Sea finds. The tapping of natural resources, such as hydro-electric power, has a similar effect. Clearly, there is not much we can do if there are no natural resources, but we can always be on the lookout for them. At the time of writing there is substantial exploration for more oil, gas and coal, both on and off-shore, and much research into generating electricity using tides, waves and winds. Perhaps we should stand all the country's economists in front of a giant windmill. The hot air produced should generate enough electricity to light up a medium-sized city.

More capital resources
Capital resources can be increased more easily. By saving more, and investing the savings in factories and machines, we should be able to produce more. One reason for the success of Japan's economy is the very high savings ratio. Unlike us, the Japanese don't like spending money. Indeed, instead of credit cards, they have debit cards! These are cards where you pay in advance for the purchasing power of the card, instead of paying later. The Japanese save and invest about 30% of their national income. British saving and investment rarely rises above 20% and is often a lot less.

We are a bit better at improving the quality of our capital resources. The quality of machinery depends on the technology involved. British scientists often make important breakthroughs in production techniques, for example in the field of computers.

Improved production techniques mean we can get more output
from fewer resources. This makes each item cheaper and easier to
sell, so that the economy both consumes more and produces more.
New technology also enables industry to improve the quality of the
product itself, or even to invent new products. Electronic calculators,
video recorders and microwave ovens are all recent examples.

More labour resources
Labour resources can be improved by increasing the size of the
working population. This is not very easy in practice. We could
make people start work at a younger age or retire later. On the
other hand, untrained youngsters and old people are not as effective. There might also be some reasonable social objections to this,
since it does seem a bit Dickensian to say the least. Alternatively,
we could encourage families to have more children. The trouble
with this is that families may not want more children; two or three
are enough for most parents. Also, it takes twenty years or so for a
policy like that to work because you have to wait for the extra kids
to grow up. A further difficulty is that, if the population rises, then
the output of the economy has to be shared out among more
people and each person gets less. In short, increasing the population is not a very attractive option. The other way to improve
labour resources is to have more education and training. Skilled
and intelligent workers are usually more productive. The quantity
and quality of goods and services produced is likely to rise as a
result. Successful economies like those of West Germany and
Japan seem to have a great deal of education and training.

More spirit of enterprise
The only other resource is enterprise. If we could encourage more
of the population to become entrepreneurs and set up businesses,
there could be a big increase in the potential output of goods and
services. Education and training may be the key to improving
enterprise, as with labour. People need to learn about commerce
and business in schools and universities. The rest of us also need to
be educated, since social attitudes have long been a big obstacle to
business in the UK. Business people have often been looked down
upon with jealous contempt. We have to realise that every business start-up not only promises to make the entrepreneur rich; it
also promises to provide some of the unemployed with jobs.

Fortunately, the anti-business ethic seems to have reversed
during the 1980s under the Thatcher Government. It is debatable
whether the Government itself has done much to foster the 'enter-

prise culture' it talks so much about. The main factor may well be
the mass unemployment resulting from its insistence that companies had to stand on their own feet without handouts from the
state. The end of Government support sent many inefficient firms
under, resulting in massive unemployment. The jobless decided,
in many cases, that self-employment was the only employment
they were ever likely to get. Many had substantial redundancy
payments to use as start-up capital. The number of new businesses
registered each year virtually doubled during the 1980s, adding a
quarter of a million firms to the register of companies.

Future prospects for growth

Of all these suggested ways of producing more goods and services
in the economy, the last seems to be most promising. We don't
need any more labour at the moment. Indeed, we have too much
labour: we need more firms to employ it all. We could probably
use more training, but successful companies are often the best
training agencies for young people. There is no shortage of capital
or high technology in the country, either. At the moment the UK
compares quite favourably with most other countries in the league
table for growth, though growth is tailing off. Growth rates for
GDP in 1988 were as follows:

Growth in GDP (1988)		Past UK growth	
Spain	5.0%	1980	−2.5%
UK	4.5%	1981	−1.5%
Italy	3.7%	1982	+1.5%
Japan	5.7%	1983	+3.3%
West Germany	3.4%	1984	+2.5%
France	3.6%	1985	+3.6%
USA	3.9%	1986	+3.0%
		1987	+4.0%

Meanwhile, the level of GDP per person in various countries
(1987) was as follows:

Switzerland	£13,800
USA	£10,700
Japan	£ 9,900
West Germany	£ 9,800
France	£ 8,300
UK	£ 6,400
Spain	£ 3,800
Brazil	£ 1,300
India	£ 220

Unfortunately, as the UK economy continues to grow, there may be a problem of congestion because of land shortages in the South East as the economy expands. We might have to choose between more economic expansion and prosperity on the one hand, and quality of environment in the Green Belt on the other. If resources are limited we cannot have everything. There is always a cost in making any economic decision. Do we want factories and houses, or forests and cows? The Green Party are so keen on preserving the environment that they want to end economic growth altogether; rather than international trade, they want a return to self-sufficiency and 'renewable resources'. Meanwhile, the Americans have just announced plans to build a base on the Moon early next century, from where important minerals could be mined to get round the problem of using up the Earth's resources.

Discussion points
1. Do we need to keep improving our living standards?
2. Should we redistribute income to underdeveloped countries?
3. Is the environment more important than economic growth?
4. Can we get economic growth without harming the environment?

RISING PRICES

We have now looked at improvements in living standards, and seen how it involves an increase in the output of real goods and services. But what if prices and wages both rise *without* any increase in the output of real goods and services? Are we better off? True, there is more money circulating around the system, but the economy is not producing any more than before. There is no *real* improvement in living standards if this happens. A general rise in all prices (including wages—the price of labour) is called **inflation**.

Why is inflation a problem?
Obviously, inflation is not generally beneficial, but is it particularly bad? Governments in the West have usually assumed that it is. Clearly, if prices and wages rise, without more output of real goods and services, the value of money must have fallen. People are simply spending more money on the same number of products. If it takes more pounds to buy something, then each pound must be worth less than it was before. Result?—savers lose out and

borrowers gain. Savers could find that their savings do not keep their true value, while borrowers may find that their debts are smaller. This could discourage saving, and mean less finance for investment in business activity. However, in some countries, like Brazil (where inflation has been around 500% for years on end), they just get around this by having extremely high interest rates (around 550%). It seems that, given time, an economy *can* adapt to inflation, even if it is very high. Everyone may simply anticipate the changes and act accordingly. In Brazil, for example, all workers claim 500% pay rises. Companies all put their prices up by 500%; and every so often they knock a couple of zeros off their bank notes.

There are some problems, however. In some cases inflation has proved to be fairly constant (as in Brazil), but in Western economies, the inflation of the 1970s tended to be variable and unpredictable. The uncertainty often meant that people tried to out-guess inflation. Workers claimed very large wage rises, more than the rate of inflation, and firms put up their prices excessively, also by more than inflation. Inflation thus tended to escalate. Accelerating inflation could, theoretically, run right out of control as it did in Germany in the 1920s: prices went up by the minute and workers were literally paid in wheelbarrows-full of virtually worthless paper money. In this situation you'd better pay for your doner kebab before it's cooked, because by the time it's done, the price will have gone up. This is called **hyper-inflation**. When this situation is reached, money ceases to be an effective medium of exchange or means of payment. Once money cannot operate effectively, an economy is reduced to barter, or commodity money, like cigarettes (see page 51). The end result is less commerce and trade, and so less output and employment—in short, severe falls in living standards.

Even if hyper-inflation does not develop, the uncertainty about inflation and possible Government action to cure it can frighten business people away from new investment. If they cannot be confident about their business venture, they may not risk doing it in the first place. This again tends to reduce commerce and trade, and with it output and employment. Finally, inflation involves more administrative costs. Sellers have to keep changing prices, perhaps printing and advertising new price lists regularly. Consumers may decide to keep all their money in high interest-paying deposits in the bank or building society, just taking out a bit at a time (because money would lose its value quickly). You might spend much of the week running to the bank and back again, at considerable trouble and expense (the 'shoe-leather costs' of inflation).

Causes of inflation

A product can experience a price change if the demand for, and supply of, that product changes. For instance, if people's demand for jelly babies becomes stronger, then they will be willing to pay a higher price. Alternatively, if the supply of jelly babies is drastically reduced because of a fire at the jelly baby warehouse, the sellers can afford to charge a higher price, since they don't have to sell as many. However, variations in particular markets of this sort would not change the general level of prices much on average. A rise in the general level of prices (inflation) can be caused in one of two ways.

- **Demand-pull inflation**

  The first type of inflation occurs when consumers are too anxious to buy things: prices are pulled up by heavy demand for the goods. Suppose the Government gives us all a big tax cut and we dash off to spend 'loadsamoney' on the latest gadgets at Dixons. Firms can't increase their output of goods and services overnight to accommodate us, because it all takes time to organise. If they have lots of customers competing to buy, and cannot produce more goods to sell, the firms will simply raise their prices. This is because, with more customers, they can afford to charge more and still sell their stock. The monetarists (page 82) believe all this can only happen if the Government prints too much money, so that there is 'too much money chasing too few goods'. Certainly, if we are going to spend more money, we need to have more money or credit available. In the early 1970s the Government allowed the supply of money and credit to expand and this helped to fuel inflation. Too much spending power leads to excessive demand from consumers, and this is what drives the price up. Inflation of this type is called **demand-pull** inflation.

- **Cost-push inflation**

  The other type of inflation occurs when firms experience an increase in their running costs and so charge higher prices to cover it. Perhaps the price of oil has gone up, making electricity more expensive. This is what happened in 1974 and again in 1979. In this case, nearly all firms will find it more expensive to run their business. Some firms, in the plastics industry, for example, will find their costs rising sharply. For inflation to occur, the rise in costs would have to affect most industries. Clearly, oil and energy costs are one example. Another possibility is an increase in the cost of labour, ie wages. If wage rates rise throughout industry, then firms will have to charge higher prices to cover their costs. Inflation caused by rising costs is called **cost-push** inflation.

The inflationary spiral

Whether inflation starts off as demand-pull or cost-push, it can quickly develop into a vicious circle. For example:

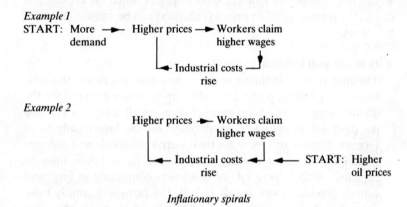

Inflationary spirals

These circles, or **inflationary spirals**, tend to get progressively worse. This is because both firms and trades unions try to stay one step ahead of inflation. If inflation is expected to be 20%, trades unions may claim 30%. Partly this is because they want a real improvement of 10% in their wages over and above inflation, and partly because of fear about what inflation will actually be. Similarly, firms may put up their prices by more than the rate of inflation to try to increase their profits, or just in case costs turn out to be rising faster than expected. Expectations of inflation can soon become self-fulfilling prophecies.

How can we cure inflation?

To cure inflation, we obviously need to reverse the causes. We could

- reduce demand to counter the demand-pull element in inflation, or
- try to hold back costs to counter the cost-push element.

If we can break the inflationary psychology, where people expect inflation and try to out-guess it, then we should be able to reverse the inflationary spiral. To do this, we have to get the rate of inflation down, eg from 20% to 10%, so that the expectations of firms and unions are reduced too.

To reduce total demand the Government must make sure that there is less consumer spending in the economy. A forced reduction in total spending is called **deflation**. This can be done in various ways.

1. The simplest would be for the Government itself to spend less on roads, schools, police, and other public services. The economic demand for all sorts of things like buildings, textbooks, jeeps and so on, would be reduced.

2. Alternatively, the Government can squeeze personal spending by increasing taxes. This would take money out of the hands of consumers, leaving them with less to spend. In either case we would end up with less money in circulation, and so less spending.

3. The Government can also tinker with the supply of money quite directly. For example it can borrow money, by selling Government bonds (gilts) to the banks or the general public. If the money borrowed is kept out of circulation rather than spent, the amount left in the economy for spending is reduced.

The problem is that any reduction in total demand in the economy is bound to upset someone. If the Government spends less on education, will fewer parents and teachers vote for them in future? If people have to pay more tax they will have less money to spend on cars, black puddings, or whatever else they enjoy. There is also bound to be unemployment: after all, if people are buying less, firms will need to produce less. If firms are producing less, they will need fewer workers to produce it.

The best solution to cost pressures is for firms to improve their efficiency (productivity per worker), in other words to produce more with the same workforce. Cost per unit of output therefore falls and this dampens cost-push inflation. The dilemma for the Government is whether or not to try to help firms, for instance by giving investment grants for new machinery. The Thatcher philosophy is that state aid to industry merely encourages firms to become dependent on the Government, and less able to cope on their own; the problem then just keeps coming back. If the Government insists that firms stand on their own two feet, then either they do, or else they go bankrupt. Many companies did improve their efficiency in response to the Government's policies in the early 1980s, but many others went bankrupt.

There are also industries where businessmen are reluctant to invest because of fluctuations in the market and the large scale of operations. Britain's building materials industry, for example, failed to invest enough in the early 1980s, and so lacked the capacity to supply the building boom of the late 1980s; billions of pounds of business went abroad. The new enterprise culture has put downward pressure on costs indirectly. More enterprise means more firms, and more competition; when firms are competing with each other they try to cut costs so that they can get business by charging lower prices.

For the Government to control industrial costs directly is hard. After all, many important costs are simply beyond its control. In the case of oil, the price is effectively decided by the Organisation of Petroleum Exporting Countries (OPEC). Wage costs, on the other hand, can be kept under control by introducing some kind of pay policy. This usually involves an upper limit on pay rises, say 5% or £10 per week. There are problems with this, however. It becomes difficult for firms in successful and expanding industries to offer higher wages to attract extra workers. Successful and expanding industries need extra workers because the demand for their products is rising. If the workers need special skills, offering a higher wage may be the only way to encourage people to train for those skills. Another problem is that unions resent having to restrain their pay claims, and often won't stand for it after a while. Once the unions have broken through the Government's limit, there is usually a mad scramble to make up for the previous low level of pay settlements. This was what happened during the 'winter of discontent' in 1979.

Inflation in the UK

Tight control of consumers' demand, while encouraging more efficiency and enterprise on the supply side, seems to be the best answer. However, Governments tend to shy away from controlling demand, particularly if heavy deflation is needed. If people sense that the Government is being soft on inflation, they start to expect inflation. We saw earlier that inflationary expectations can be self-fulfilling. On the other hand, if the Government is brave enough to take a tough stand on consumer demand in the beginning, this can create expectations of low inflation, so that people do not scramble to claim higher wages, or to put up prices. Public perceptions about the Government's attitude are crucial: the Thatcher Government appears to have had until 1989 a reasonably solid inflation-fighting image.

Despite rising inflation during 1988 and 1989, the UK's inflation performance during the 1980s has been passable, as shown by the following comparisons:

UK inflation

1981	11.0%
1982	8.0%
1983	5.0%
1984	4.7%
1985	5.9%
1986	3.5%
1987	4.0%
1988	4.9%
1989	7.1% (estimated)

World inflation 1988 (1989 estimate in brackets)

Japan	0.7% (3.0%)
West Germany	1.2% (3.0%)
France	2.7% (3.5%)
USA	4.1% (5.2%)
Italy	5.0% (5.8%)

Discussion points
1. Why do ordinary people dislike inflation?
2. Why do we tend to get more inflation just *after* an election (eg 1975, 1980, 1988)?
3. Who suffers most when there is inflation?

JOBS AND UNEMPLOYMENT

Jobs are created when firms hire workers. There is no reason in a Western economy why the number of jobs created should be the same as the number of people wishing to work. Anyone is free to start up a business and to employ others. However, there is no guarantee that enough people will be running enough businesses to employ the entire workforce. When there are workers willing and able to work, but who cannot find jobs, we say there is **unemployment**.

There are several types of unemployment and various policies which can be adopted to cure the problem. At present, unemployment clearly is a problem. From an economic point of view unemployment means wasted resources. The economy is not producing as much as it could, and so the material standard of living is not as high as it could be. Many social problems are associated with unemployment; crime, divorce and suicide for example all increase during a period of high unemployment.

What causes unemployment?

The most obvious cause of unemployment is people temporarily moving between jobs. When there are plenty of jobs available workers often leave one job before they find another. There are also workers who have been made redundant, perhaps because their firm is closing down. They may be unemployed temporarily while they search for a new job. Temporary unemployment of this sort is called **frictional unemployment**. Since it is temporary it is not a serious problem. There are also some people who are **unemployables**, for example because of physical or mental handicap, illiteracy or criminality. These people are few in number, relatively speaking, and it is difficult to do much about them.

More worrying is **structural unemployment**. This occurs when large pockets of unemployment develop in a particular place. Such blackspots are usually caused by the decline of a particular industry in a town which had relied heavily upon it. It could happen, for instance, if natural resources run out or become expensive to mine, as in the case of Cornish tin. Another explanation is rapid automation in an industry. Robots have now replaced most of the Midlands car workers. There may also be a sudden rush of cheap imports from abroad (far eastern clothing undermined the Lancashire textile industry). Structural unemployment poses problems for a particular region, but not for the economy as a whole.

Yet more serious is **mass unemployment**: there simply isn't enough economic activity in the country as a whole to employ everyone. This is a nationwide problem. Mass unemployment can result if there is too little demand for products in the economy by consumers. Perhaps the Government is taking too much money in taxes, or failing to spend enough money itself. Or, perhaps there are too few domestic firms or the firms are not producing enough to employ everyone. A lack of production may be caused by a shortage of good entrepreneurs or by lack of investment in industrial capacity. Or it may be that foreign firms can produce things more cheaply, so that domestic firms cannot compete. Home firms would be expensive if workers kept getting big pay increases or if they were not carefully managed. Another reason for mass employment might be a world recession: economic activity and incomes are low throughout the world. This would obviously reduce trade and so there would be less output, with fewer workers needed.

How can we reduce unemployment?

To cure unemployment, we would have to reverse the causes discussed above. We have already said that it is difficult to do much about **unemployables**, and that temporary or **frictional unemployment** between jobs is not a serious problem; indeed, high levels of frictional unemployment can be a sign of a healthy economy. People are more willing to leave one job before they find another when there are plenty of jobs to be had in an economy.

Structural unemployment is very hard to deal with. If an area is in economic decline, can we persuade the workers to move away to take up jobs in more prosperous areas? Easy enough, you might think, when they are living in depressed areas. However, this destroys communities and also leads to difficulties over amenities. Roads, schools, hospitals, homes and so on are called the **infrastructure**. If people migrate then the infrastructure they leave behind goes to waste. Meanwhile the infrastructure in the areas they move to has to cope with too heavy a burden. A better solution is to try to persuade new firms in other industries to enter areas of high unemployment. They may do this of their own accord if there is plenty of labour and the workers are willing to work for a low wage (which they probably will be if there aren't any jobs). Alternatively, the Government could try to tempt the firms with grants or other incentives.

If there is **mass unemployment** the only answer is to try and increase the level of economic activity—a bigger output of goods and services. The measures we discussed on page 87 for creating growth will create more jobs in the process. More demand by consumers means that firms try to produce more, and then more workers have to be employed. The output of firms can also increase if they improve their efficiency. For example if they invest in new machinery, they can produce more cheaply and attract more customers. Once again, more workers will be taken on.

One of the most effective ways of creating new jobs is to encourage **new enterprise**. Instead of trying to expand existing firms, we could make it easier for people to set up their own businesses. Each new enterprise takes at least one person off the dole and, if successful, more. Education can be an important weapon in generating more enterprise. The support of the Government for small and new businesses is also crucial. Paradoxically, mass unemployment can be a help in this respect. When there are millions unemployed, finding a job can be almost impossible. In this case, people may be driven to start up their own businesses. This is particularly likely if workers have been given redundancy pay, which can often be many thousands of pounds.

When trying to cure unemployment by increasing economic activity we should not allow wage rates to rise too fast. If labour becomes expensive, then even expanding firms may be reluctant to take workers on. Machines may prove to be cheaper than people, and machines don't ask for a pay rise. (Machines are not always more economical, however; it depends on how much the workers are getting paid.) Certainly, firms are more likely to employ people when the wage rate stays low than if it rises.

What the unemployment statistics mean

The actual method of counting the unemployment statistics varies from place to place and time to time. In the 1980s there were several changes to the way UK unemployment statistics were presented. The most controversial was the change in 1980, which excluded married women. Married women who are looking for work do not claim unemployment benefit because their husbands will either be working or claiming unemployment benefit themselves. The Government argued that since these women had husbands who were earning or claiming, they could not be classed as unemployed. Apart from being blatantly sexist, this is economically unsound. A married woman who is willing and able to work, but is not in a job, still represents a wasted resource. These women could be producing goods and services and are not doing so.

Besides dubious Government tinkering of this sort, there are other more acceptable modifications. The figures have to be **seasonally adjusted**. This is because unemployment always changes at certain times of the year. For instance in September:

- school leavers can start claiming benefit;
- people employed in seaside summer work lose their jobs.

Suppose unemployment usually rises by 50,000 in September because of these seasonal events. If actual unemployment one September rises by 70,000, then 50,000 of this rise is accounted for by 'seasonal factors' and the remaining 20,000 is the 'true' rise in unemployment for that month. The seasonally adjusted figure is therefore up by only 20,000.

Assessing unemployment in the UK

The unemployment position in the UK became particularly serious in the early 1980s because of world recession and the Government's deflationary policies, designed to cure inflation. However, since the summer of 1986 there has been a big fall in the measured level of unemployment. This reflects improved economic growth in the UK during the 1980s as a result of new enterprise, and a steady recovery in world trade. Compared with the recent past and with many of our competitors, our employment position is not too bad. Consider the following statistics:

Selected unemployment figures 1988

Spain	19.0%	of workforce
Italy	12.5%	
Belgium	10.8%	
France	10.7%	
Netherlands	10.0%	
UK	7.6%	
West Germany	6.0%	
USA	6.0%	
Japan	2.7%	

UK unemployment record

1979	6.0%
1980	7.7%
1981	11.1%
1982	12.8%
1983	12.9%
1984	13.4%
1985	13.2%

Adult unemployment only from 1986

1986	11.4%
1987	9.4%
1988	7.6%
1989	6.0%

Discussion points

1. Does everyone have a right to a job? Does this mean that someone owes you a living?
2. Why is unemployment higher in some places than in others?
3. How serious are the social problems caused by unemployment?

4. Are there any advantages to high unemployment?

THE DISTRIBUTION OF INCOME

Economists refer to a **labour market**, where firms 'buy' and workers 'sell' labour. The wage or salary paid to a worker represents the 'price' of labour. Like any other market left to its own devices, the labour market will settle out at an equilibrium price, or wage. The size of the equilibrium price in any market depends on the strength of demand and supply in that market (see page 23). In the same way, the wage or salary paid in the labour market depends on the demand and supply of workers. In reality there are many different labour markets for the many different kinds of workers. Each market has different supply and demand characteristics and so ends up with a different wage or salary. This **distribution of income**, not surprisingly, is one of the most contentious issues in society. We need to analyse the factors behind the distribution of income before we can assess the rights and wrongs of the situation.

Why are there inequalities of income?

The main reason why some people earn a high wage is a **shortage** in the labour market. If lots of workers are required for a particular job and not many are available, then as in any other market, the shortage will lead to a rise in price. Shortages may arise if an industry is expanding. Suppose a new product or service is invented that consumers very much want to buy, such as a Greek ferry that runs on time. In struggling to produce enough of the service to satisfy its customers the ferry company tries to employ more and more sailors. This may create a shortage for those workers and drive up the price of labour in the ferry industry, ie the wage rate. The reverse is also true. If hardly anybody wants a particular product (say steam locomotives) then firms won't want to employ many people to make it, and there will be a surplus of workers in that labour market, keeping the wage rate low.

All this means that workers can be moved into the industries which produce the goods that consumers want. Popular goods will require expansion, and expansion of an industry creates a shortage of labour. Wages must then rise in that industry to attract more workers into it. Conversely, with goods consumers don't want, there is contraction, a surplus of labour, and wages stay down to encourage workers to move elsewhere. All this helps a free market system to work efficiently. The same process ensures that if there happen to be the wrong number of people trying to work in a particular industry, there will be a sensible adjustment. If everyone suddenly decided they wanted to be computer operators, there would be a surplus of computer operators; this would drive down the wage rate and workers would leave the industry for something better paid elsewhere. If nobody felt like being a computer operator, there would be a shortage of computer workers. The shortage would drive up the wage rate and workers would enter the industry. Thus, the wage rate moves (over a period of time) to ensure equilibrium in the various labour markets, just like the price in any other market.

Another key factor in deciding earnings is **effort**. Workers who make more effort produce more. Firms are therefore willing to pay them more for their services. This is easy to see if wages are paid by the hours of work done. Equally, sales representatives are paid a commission based on how much they sell. Setting up your own business is another example of making an effort, and here the potential rewards can be very great if the business succeeds.

It is worth noting that a successful business employs other people besides the entrepreneur who sets it up. The business and its workers also pay tax to the Government so that society as a whole also benefits. It might be argued that sometimes people get money for nothing, for instance by earning interest on savings, or rent on property. Such income is in a sense 'unearned', but we have to give people with surplus capital and property an incentive to loan out what they have to others who can use it productively. Thus interest and rent are essential parts of a free market system, and part of the process of income distribution.

A further reason for having to pay higher wages in some industries is that the job is unattractive. Working on a building site or oil rig brings with it the risk of serious injury or death, and some teachers are only marginally safer. In these cases we have to pay more to attract the workers. The fatality rate for divers in the North Sea is incredibly high. In addition, most men don't like having to spend weeks at a time on a metal box in the middle of the ocean without any women. The wage rate for rig workers is therefore very high indeed. This all seems quite reasonable. Without high wages in unpleasant conditions, we might never get anyone to do important jobs. Indeed there have frequently been cases of labour shortages for this reason, as in the case of nurses and teachers. Aside from pure economics, it also seems fair to pay more to people if they do unpleasant or hazardous jobs.

Another reason why some people tend to get paid more, is that they have acquired an **education** or **training**. This is for two reasons:

- Educated and trained workers are usually more productive and so firms are willing to pay more for their services. An untrained car mechanic wouldn't be much use; and, to take an extreme example, it wouldn't be very productive to have an untrained surgeon performing operations.

- Education and training itself is often long, hard, boring and underpaid. To persuade young people to do it we have to hold out the prospect of higher pay later on, otherwise few people would bother. In the end we wouldn't have enough car mechanics, doctors and so on, and everyone would want jobs that need no formal qualifications at all, like being Princess of Wales, or Chancellor of the Exchequer.

A more contentious reason for higher pay is **ability**. If someone is particularly able in their field—whether car mechanics or brain surgery—they will tend to get more money. An able person is more productive, and it pays a firm to offer more money to keep his services. This is why prized staff can often ask for pay rises. The more able people are often the ones who set up successful businesses and make huge profits. The rights and wrongs of this are debateable. Clearly, a person who is very able can produce more than someone who is not, and he doesn't have to make more effort in order to do it. So the amount of work needed for a genius to set up a thriving business may be less than the amount of work needed by a street sweeper. The problem with this sort of argument is that we have to give the able person an incentive. If we said that everyone would be paid the same, regardless of how much they produced, nobody would produce very much. Able people would just produce the same as everyone else, though with less effort. Imagine what would happen if I told my students that they would all get a grade B regardless of what they did. I expect that neither the weak ones nor the clever ones would do any work at all, since they would have nothing to gain.

And then, finally we have **luck**. If you win money on the pools most people don't mind. If you inherit it from wealthy parents everybody hates you. Presumably this is because we all had an equal chance of winning the pools. But of course, people who complain, either about pools winnings or about inheritance, are usually just jealous. The incentive argument is important here too. Able people who start successful businesses (which employ others) often do so for the sake of their children. Banning inheritance may remove some of the reason for making an effort. In any case, ability itself is at least partly inherited, so children of successful people are more likely to be successful. This may be unfair but there doesn't seem to be much we can do about it, short of starving clever children of oxygen to induce brain-damage and/or taking them away from their parents to prevent money and knowledge from being passed on. Luck can also work in other ways. Workers who are lucky enough to be part of a powerful trade union can often negotiate high wages. This was the case with miners and electricity workers in the 1970s. The fact that they had more industrial muscle did not make it 'fair' for these people to receive more pay than say nurses.

The Government and income distribution

The Government can, of course, also influence the distribution of income. It does this in two ways:

- it can **tax** people
- it can give handouts (**benefits**) to people.

If the Government disapproves of the distribution of income it can change things using taxes and benefits. Usually, the Government takes taxes from the rich and gives handouts to the poor (I assume most of us agree that it ought to be this way around). We need to decide what a reasonable distribution of income actually is, and how far the present distribution differs from the one we want. Having done all that, we will also have to decide the best economic method to try to achieve the income distribution we want.

The 'best' income distribution depends on your point of view. It is surely important to check the income level at the bottom end. If income is unevenly distributed but the poorest people are still comfortable, this is obviously not as much of a problem as if the poorest were in a very bad state. In other words, we need to consider the total size of the cake as well as how to share it out. In the UK the poorest people are looked after through the benefits system. The most serious problems for poorer people are a chronic shortage of adequate housing, and the very long National Health Service waiting lists.

If people need incentives to make an effort and to start their own businesses, it seems that some inequality is actually needed to achieve national prosperity. People who work harder—particularly those who start up businesses—need to be encouraged. This increases output and employment in the economy (growth). It also allows the Government to collect more in taxes to provide services for the needy. As a result everyone benefits, though obviously the successful business person benefits most. The desire of some intellectuals to stifle free enterprise smacks of cutting off your nose to spite your face. After all, it is the poorest and weakest people who lose most when the economy stagnates through lack of initiative and enterprise; the able and successful can always take care of themselves.

A further difficulty in an advanced society is the question, what constitutes a 'minimum acceptable' standard of living? In the modern developed world, we want to give the poor *more* than just enough to avoid starvation. We want to ensure that they have decent housing, health and education, perhaps even a little left over for entertainment. This raises social and economic issues of great concern to both the rich, whose taxes are paying for the handouts, and the poor, who receive the benefits.

The Thatcher Government has placed great emphasis on the 'enterprise culture'. This has succeeded in improving the average standard of living. However, there seems to be a feeling in the country that the Government should now put more resources into public services for those who are not quite so enterprising and successful. Public concern over education and health services is growing, and the Government's success at generating new enterprise has led to a rapid expansion in tax revenues. The problem for the Government is to keep the lid on inflation. Spending more on health and education would unfortunately increase total demand and put upward pressure on prices (see earlier page 93 on inflation). Meanwhile, the thriving businesses of the 1980s have increased inequality in UK incomes, as shown below:

Share of total UK income (after tax/benefits)

	1975	1985
Bottom tenth of population:	3.0%	2.7%
Top tenth of population:	23.1%	26.5%

Discussion points
1. Is the distribution of income more important than the level of income?
2. Is equality in income a practical possibility?
3. What sort of needs should be covered by Government benefits?
4. What is a 'fair' level of income tax?

5

The International Economy

FOREIGN TRADE

Trade with other countries can greatly benefit any economy. There are several reasons for this, which we shall look at in a moment. While trying to encourage sales to foreigners, most countries also try to keep foreign goods out. These rather contradictory policies also need to be discussed.

Why trade pays

Specialisation
One of the main advantages for nations who trade with each other is **specialisation**. Suppose that the UK and Greece can both produce wine and both produce whisky. Let's say that the British are better at producing whisky than the Greeks, while the Greeks are better at producing wine than the British. By 'better' we mean that the British can produce more whisky per man-hour of work than the Greeks, and vice versa for wine. Therefore, if the Greeks specialise in producing wine, and the British in whisky, we should get more whisky and more wine. If the two countries specialise, whisky only gets produced by the British (who can make a lot of it per man-hour of work) and wine only gets produced by the Greeks (who can make a lot of it per man-hour of work). We therefore end up with more of both products than we would get if each country has to make some whisky and some wine. But, of course, if Greece and the UK specialise but do not trade with each other, the British will only have whisky to drink and the Greeks will only have wine. This would be a rather boring way of getting drunk. So they are only likely to want to specialise if they can trade whisky for wine afterwards to get a bit of both products. Trade is therefore important if countries are to gain the benefits of specialisation without losing out on the products they don't specialise in.

Economies of scale

Once a country has specialised in certain products, it tends to produce a lot of those products. Large scale production leads to **economies of scale** or cost savings due to size (see page 44). There are cost savings through bulk buying, improved use of machinery and so on. People also tend to get better at a certain activity if they do a lot of it for a long time (with the possible exception of English cricket). A country may develop a good reputation for something it does a lot of, for example champagne in France, or banking in the City of London. Obviously, not every town could manufacture its own cars; one large car factory for the whole country is better because of economies of scale. Following the same line of argument, why should every country manufacture its own cars, or its own steel? Why shouldn't countries specialise in certain goods the way towns do? But, of course, countries will only specialise if they can trade afterwards to get the products other countries produce.

Spin-off business

There are other advantages to free trade between countries as well. A whole range of industries and services are linked to international trade. Because of trade between countries, there is business for shipping lines, employing sailors and dockers. The ships have to be built and this employs thousands more people. Someone has to provide insurance for the shipment and arrange foreign currency dealings to finance it, which results in yet more employment. As you can see, trade has a big effect on the world economy as a whole.

Cheaper goods and services

More foreign trade also means more **competition** in selling things to consumers. Competition is important because it means that firms have to attract consumers through lower prices. If a big British firm dominates the home market for a particular product, it may be able to get away with a high price, since consumers have little choice but to buy from it. Opening up the market to foreign companies gives consumers the option not to buy from the British firm. The British firm may then be forced to cut its price to keep its customers; it will need to reduce its costs by improving efficiency. We could end up with a more economical use of resources, which would benefit the nation as a whole. Competition also encourages firms to provide a better service. It was no coincidence that British Telecom suddenly discovered how to make push-button telephones after 1980 when other firms were allowed to compete with it for the first time.

Worldwide choice of goods and services
There are many products which some countries cannot make at all. To take a simple example, the British cannot make pineapples and bananas, while some tropical countries can't make much else *but* pineapples and bananas. If Britain did not trade with them, these countries could not sell all those pineapples and bananas to their own citizens; there is a limit to how many bananas you can eat. This means that there would be fewer jobs for plantation workers in those tropical countries. At the same time, of course, the British would have less choice of food available to them.

For countries that cannot produce certain items, trade helps both employment and consumer satisfaction. The same applies even when a country can make the products itself. The British can produce high fashion wear, but the availability of French and Italian fashions gives the consumers a much wider choice and a chance to find something they really like.

Why is trade controlled?
Most countries would prefer to sell lots of things to foreigners while not buying too many themselves. There are two reasons for this:

- **Financial:** goods bought from other countries have to be paid for; goods sold to other countries bring money in.
- **Employment:** if we can sell lots of things abroad, this increases output and employment in Britain. If we buy lots of things from abroad this reduces output and employment in Britain. If consumers buy Japanese cars, then fewer British made cars will be needed and there will be less British employment.

Because of all this countries play various dirty tricks to try to encourage the sale of goods abroad while discouraging foreign goods from coming in. They are specially keen to keep out foreign goods when there is a big industry for those goods at home, an industry which might find its products harder to sell as a result of foreign competition.

How can we boost sales to foreigners? The simplest way is through a Government subsidy. This means giving firms a cash handout when they sell something abroad (the European Community does this for its farmers), or giving a tax credit to firms who sell abroad (VAT does not have to be collected on goods sold abroad, for instance). You cannot, of course, *force* foreigners to buy your goods, but Governments can provide help for selling abroad. This help can range from free advice and information to financial guarantees for foreign currency dealings.

The array of weapons for stopping goods coming in from abroad is more impressive. After all, Governments are then playing on their home ground. An obvious weapon is a **tax** on foreign goods coming into the country. Such taxes are called **tariffs** or **customs duties**. These work by making the foreign product more expensive, to discourage home consumers from buying it. Alternatively, if the foreign producers keep the price down, they themselves get much less, since some of the price paid by consumers goes to the Government in tax.

If people are so keen to buy Japanese goods that they will pay an even higher price, we can still control things by simply making it illegal to import more than a certain number each year. In the case of cars, we have a **voluntary export agreement** with the Japanese. This means they 'volunteer' not to sell us more than 20,000 cars a year (otherwise we ban them altogether).

There are various more subtle ways of discouraging foreign goods. We can use bureaucracy at the point of entry. All Japanese video recorders are forced to go through the same customs post in France. All the paperwork means that only a limited number can get through each year. The Germans impose very strict safety standards, so that some foreign companies cannot get a licence to sell in Germany (or can only do so after expensive modifications to their products).

Problems with trade controls

The problem with all these controls is that they discourage trade. Less trade means less of all the advantages of trade which we discussed earlier. The effect on the world economy as a whole of more controls and less trade could be very harmful. If one country starts imposing restrictions, other countries are likely to retaliate. During the recession of the 1930s many countries tried to protect their home industries by restricting the sale of foreign goods in various ways. As countries began to retaliate against each other, the trade war escalated. In the end, the recession was much worse than it might have been. All the trade that had been lost meant huge reductions in output and jobs in many countries. We saw before that there are many goods which can only be bought and sold abroad. Obstructing this trade simply leads to less economic activity, since consumers have no home-produced alternatives. All the linked industries, such as shipping and international finance, suffer too. Consumers suffer most because of the reduced output, reduced competition and reduced choice.

However, a case can sometimes be made for having controls on foreign goods coming in. If a country has a very large economy relative to other countries, as in the USA for instance, it can affect the world price of the goods it buys abroad. When millions of Americans are clamouring to buy Japanese cameras, say, this makes a big difference to the market for Japanese cameras. It increases the demand in that market quite substantially. Whenever there are lots of customers and demand is high the price is likely to rise (see page 20), so it may not be in the large economy's interest to allow totally free buying of foreign goods. Theoretically, imposing a tariff could reduce American demand for Japanese cameras until the price is no longer pulled up. Also, the threat of retaliation works less well for a large economy like the USA. In a trade war with a smaller country the USA would lose far less than the other country. This is because the USA, being a large market, is more important to the other country trying to sell goods abroad than the other country, being a small market, is to the US. This makes the Americans very hard to deal with in trade negotiations.

Small **less developed nations** can also make a case for imposing controls on foreign imports. Indeed, if they want their industries to develop they may have to do this. In heavy manufacturing industries, there are important economies of scale. The established foreign producers already have these economies of scale, while the local industry which is in its infancy is not yet big enough to get them. In a free trade situation, the established large firms from abroad will be able to charge a lower price than the fledgeling firms at home. This could strangle the infant industries before they have a chance to grow up.

Other arguments for tariffs also exist. They may help protect an ancient industry or craft which is less efficient than a more modern industry abroad. Allowing some old industries to die may destroy a whole way of life. For instance, closing coal mines which produce coal costing more than foreign coal would destroy the mining villages. If we import food into Europe from outside because Mediterranean farming is inefficient and therefore expensive, Mediterranean farming communities will be destroyed. Even if we accept the need to preserve a traditional way of life, there are cheaper ways of doing it. We could dispense with tariffs and just pay those communities subsidies to enable them keep going.

There may also be some strategic arguments for keeping an

industry going even when its foreign competitors are cheaper. This could apply to industries which make, or could make, hardware for war including shipbuilding and car production. This argument is obviously liable to be abused. Some other arguments don't work at all. For example, it has been said that far eastern labour is cheap, giving them an 'unfair' advantage. In the case of Japan this just isn't true. In the case of Korea or Taiwan, they have few choices about how to earn a living, and so will work for a low wage. Their economy is, after all, under-developed. If we don't buy their goods then, instead of working for a low wage, they don't work at all, so we certainly won't be doing them any favours. We won't be helping ourselves either. Specialisation increases total world output, which makes us all better off as we explained earlier. Perhaps we should leave them to make clothes and electrical goods, while we concentrate on the things we are best at, like chemicals and financial services.

Discussion points
1. Should we prevent people from buying foreign goods?
2. Should we prevent foreigners from buying control of British companies?
3. Should we prevent foreign firms from setting up factories here?

THE BALANCE OF PAYMENTS AND THE EXCHANGE RATE

The **balance of payments** accounts measure the value of a country's trade with other countries. The **exchange rate** is the rate that you get when you swap your currency for another country's currency. These two things are closely connected and we shall be examining the relationship between them. We shall also be considering the factors which affect the balance of payments and the exchange rate.

Balance of payments accounts
The balance of payments accounts are in three main sections, as follows:

> A. The current account
>   — Visibles
>   — Invisibles
> B. The capital account
> C. Official financing

For each section there are credit items (money coming into the country to pay for things we produce), and debit items (money going out of the country to pay for things foreigners produce abroad). In the case of the current account visibles, we are talking about goods: things you can see. Credits arise when we sell goods to foreigners and they pay us. These are **exports**. Debits arise when we buy things from foreigners and we pay them. These are **imports**. Current account invisibles are intangible services, such as international insurance or tourism. Credits on the invisibles account are exports of these services to foreigners; debits are imports of these services from foreigners. The capital account measures flows of money for investment purposes. For example, people may wish to invest in overseas property or shares, or simply deposit money in overseas banks to take advantage of high interest rates.

The overall balance of credits and debits, on both the current account and the capital account taken together, is the **balance of payments**. Whatever it comes to, the Government has to finance it. This Government finance is counted in the official financing section of the accounts.

- **Balance of payments deficit**

  Suppose all the debits exceed all the credits by £100 million. The country as a whole therefore owes foreigners £100 million more for imports than it has earned from exports. This debt has to be paid and the Bank of England pays it out of reserves of foreign currencies. It could also borrow foreign currencies from foreign banks.

- **Balance of payments surplus**

  Alternatively, if credits exceed debits and foreigners owe us money, then the Bank of England will be receiving foreign currencies, which it can add to its reserves. It could also use the foreign currencies to pay off debts or to make loans to foreign countries.

The most commonly quoted figure in the media is the **current account** balance. Although a large deficit on current account looks like a problem, it need not be. True, if imports exceed exports on current account we owe foreigners money. But if, at the same time, **capital** flowing into the country exceeds capital flowing out, then the *overall* balance of payments may not be in the red. Foreign capital flowing into the country provides foreign currency

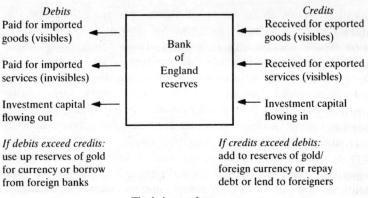

The balance of payments

which can be used to pay off debts on the current account. This tactic cannot be kept up for long, however. Capital flowing in for investment will go into property, shares or bank deposits. These investments all involve a certain payment in return, namely rent, dividends and interest. If we have lots of good capital inflows now, in future years we will unfortunately have lots of these return payments to make.

Payments in return for foreign investment are counted in the current account invisibles section of the balance of payments. So if a current account deficit is financed by capital inflows, the current account deficit will actually get worse in the future. The Government may therefore prefer to finance any current account deficit itself. But, of course, if it does so out of its reserves of foreign currencies this cannot go on forever, either. Sooner or later, the Bank of England would simply run out of foreign currency reserves. The Government therefore really needs to act now to cure a current account deficit, if it is to avoid recurring financial problems in the future. Precisely what the Government can do we shall look at later on when we have looked at the factors underlying the balance of payments.

The balance of payments and the exchange rate

One crucial aspect of the balance of payments is its relationship with the exchange rate. The **exchange rate** can be thought of as the price of one currency expressed in terms of another currency. For example, the dollar exchange rate for sterling is the price of pounds expressed in dollars. Like any other price this price is established in a market place. The market we are talking about is the one in which people swap sterling for dollars and vice versa. Some people will be buying sterling with dollars, while others will be selling sterling in exchange for dollars. The price (in dollars) at which they buy and sell pounds is the exchange rate, say £1 = $1.60. The people who actually do the buying and selling on the currency markets are banks from various countries. In our example, they would be British and American banks. When they buy and sell currency, banks are usually doing so on behalf of their customers who need it for transactions involving foreign countries, such as imports and exports.

How do transactions involving foreign countries lead people to deal in foreign currencies? Suppose a British television station wanted to buy (import) an American soap opera. The importer would have to pay for it with dollars, so he would ask his bank in Britain to buy some dollars. The bank then has to sell some of his sterling in exchange for dollars on the dollar exchange market. Likewise, if someone wants to invest in American property or shares he will have to get hold of dollars first from his bank, so that the bank will end up selling sterling in exchange for dollars. On the other hand, suppose an American wants to buy Tower Bridge and take it back to the US. He will have to pay for it in pounds and ask his own American bank to get hold of sterling. The American bank will therefore end up buying sterling with dollars. The same happens if Americans want to invest in British property or shares. We therefore have sterling being *supplied* onto the foreign exchange market when British people want to buy imports from abroad or invest abroad; sterling is *demanded* in the market when foreigners are buying British exports or investing in Britain.

The actual exchange rate is established by means of the price mechanism (see page 20). The exchange rate will settle out at an equilibrium level where the supply of sterling (for imports and investment abroad) is equal to the demand for sterling (for exports and investment from abroad). If the supply of sterling exceeds the demand for it, dealers will cut their price (the exchange rate) to sell off their surplus stocks of sterling. As the price of sterling falls people become more willing to buy again and less willing to sell; a balance is restored. On the other hand if the demand for sterling is greater than the supply, dealers will bid up the price of sterling (the exchange rate) to try and get hold of the scarce supply. This will encourage more sterling to be supplied and less to be demanded, so that a balance is restored once again. In either case, the price change tends to move the market towards equilibrium by adjusting demand and supply in the right direction. The price in this case is the exchange rate; the demand comes from exports and capital inflows; the supply comes from imports and capital outflows. The exchange rate therefore depends crucially on the balance of payments position. If there is a deficit, imports and capital outflows are greater than exports and capital inflows, so the supply of sterling exceeds demand and the exchange rate falls. If there is a surplus the reverse is true.

Factors affecting the balance of payments

Let's look in more detail at the factors which affect exports and imports. The most obvious is **incomes**. If incomes in the UK are high, then people will buy lots of imports from abroad (especially from Japan at present). The result will be a balance of payments *deficit*. On the other hand, if foreigners have more money to spend, they are more likely to buy exports from us. The result would then be a balance of payments *surplus*. How do British and foreign goods compare in terms of quality and price? If our goods are reliable and cheap, we will sell lots of exports and have a balance of payments surplus. If foreign goods are even more reliable and even cheaper we will end up with lots of imports and a balance of payments deficit.

Capital flows for investment also depend on the level of incomes. The attractiveness and costs of the investments matter too. An overseas investment will be attractive if investors have confidence in the economy and if the returns on investments are likely to be high. People would not wish to invest in a war zone, for instance, because they might suddenly find that their investment is in the hands of warring armies, who might be reluctant to give it back. Investing in other countries is particularly profitable if the interest rate is higher than elsewhere. If British interest rates are higher than elsewhere, then capital will flow into Britain to be deposited in British banks, giving us a payments surplus. Conversely, if interest rates are higher elsewhere, capital will flow out of Britain and we will have a payments deficit.

A deficit on Britain's balance of payments implies lots of imports and lots of capital flowing out to be invested abroad. This means that lots of Britons will be selling their sterling in exchange for foreign currencies. The result is that the price of sterling will fall as dealers cut their prices to try to sell off the extra supplies. In other words, the exchange rate will drop, until equilibrium is restored (at a lower or cheaper exchange rate, where less sterling is supplied and more is demanded). The reverse of all this happens if there is a surplus. Lots of exports, and lots of investment from abroad, means a strong demand by foreigners for sterling; this pushes up the price of sterling until a new equilibrium is established at a higher exchange rate.

The fact that a balance of payments surplus pulls the exchange rate up, and that a deficit pushes it down, can be used to predict what will happen to the exchange rate. Currency speculators can make a profit by selling a currency when it is expensive and buying it when it is cheaper. This kind of speculation can itself affect the exchange rate. If speculators *think* that sterling is about to rise in value, they dash out to buy it. The extra demand means that the exchange rate *does* rise. Conversely, if they expect the exchange rate to fall they dash to sell, and it does fall.

The Government and the balance of payments

The Government can also intervene in all this. It can try to manipulate the balance of payments by influencing the factors which affect it. For example:

- it can put up taxes to reduce spending power to reduce imports. This would tend to create a surplus on the balance of payments, and so push up the exchange rate.
- it can put up interest rates. This will attract capital investment from abroad and help to create a surplus on payments. The surplus again pushes up the exchange rate.

The Government can also manipulate the exchange rate directly. The Bank of England can sell sterling on the foreign exchange markets to drive its value down; or it can buy up sterling with reserves of foreign currencies to increase the exchange rate of sterling. Playing around with the exchange rate will then affect the balance of payments. If the exchange rate is high, then sterling is expensive. This means it is expensive to get hold of sterling to pay for British exports. This makes exports less attractive. Imports on the other hand look cheaper, since it now takes less sterling to buy the foreign currency needed to pay for them. The result is that a balance of payments deficit is more likely in the long run. Conversely, if the exchange rate is pushed down by the Government, exports become cheaper and imports become more expensive, so that the balance of payments is likely to improve in the long run. However, although this is good for exports it can tend to cause inflation, because it makes imported goods and raw materials more expensive.

The Government may prefer a stable exchange rate that does not tend to move either up or down. Stability reduces risks and encourages business to invest in projects which involve international trade.

Assessing Britain's balance of payments

In practice, for most of the period since 1945 the British balance of payments has been weak, with imports exceeding exports. Essentially, we were importing lots of primary products (food, oil and other raw materials) and paying for them with manufactured goods and financial services—only not *quite*. Since there was often a deficit on the balance of payments, the Government had to keep devaluing sterling's exchange rate to make British exports more attractive and to discourage imports. The increase in world oil prices in 1974 put particular pressure on the balance of payments and the exchange rate.

However, the situation reversed itself dramatically in the late 1970s. When Britain began to produce North Sea oil, the high oil prices meant that we had a substantial surplus on the balance of payments. This in turn meant that sterling was much in demand by foreigners wanting to pay for British oil, and so the price of sterling rose. This increase in the exchange rate unfortunately made our exports of manufactures expensive and less competitive. By the early 1980s the balances were the other way around. Britain was a net exporter of primary goods (mainly oil) and a net importer of manufactures. Because of the immense value of oil, the overall balance was continuously in surplus in this phase, right up to 1985 (when oil prices fell again). Financial services continued to make an important contribution to our trade position in the 'invisibles' section of the current account.

Since 1985 we have steadily found ourselves suffering from the worst of all possible worlds. Much of our manufacturing trade was damaged by the high exchange rate in the early 1980s, which made exports expensive, and our oil trade has been halved in value because of the oil price collapse in 1985. At the same time, there was a massive consumer boom in the late 1980s, sucking in imports. The result was a huge and growing balance of payments deficit. This does not represent a crisis, though, since the Government accumulated very large foreign currency reserves during the surplus years. These reserves can be used to pay for the deficits while Government policies to dampen demand and restrain imports take effect. The high interest rates which are being used to control inflation and support the exchange rate also help to attract foreign money on the capital account, for deposits in UK banks.

This can also be used, temporarily, to finance the deficit while the problem is sorted out.

Our performance contrasts unfavourably with the Germans and Japanese, who have a perpetual balance of payments surplus. But we are not as bad as the Americans, who have a truly vast trade deficit which exceeds the GDP of most countries in the world.

The UK balance of payments current account

1973	−£1,089m	
1974	−£3,316m	
1975	−£1,582m	
1976	−£914m	
1977	−£128m	
1978	+£972m	
1979	−£736m	
1980	+£3,122m	
1981	+£6,936m	
1982	+£4,685m	
1983	+£3,831m	
1984	+£2,022m	
1985	+£3,338m	
1986	−£198m	
1987	−£2,504m	
1988	−£13,555m	
1989	−£20,500m	(estimate)

International current account balances in 1988

USA	−£73,000m
Japan	+£42,000m
West Germany	+£26,000m
France	−£2,000m
Italy	−£2,000m

Discussion points

1. Does it matter if the value of the pound falls?
2. Why does Britain perform better in invisible trade than visible trade?
3. Where would we be without North Sea oil?
4. What will happen to the balance of payments when North Sea oil runs out?

INTERNATIONAL ORGANISATIONS

There are several organisations connected with international trade. The most important for the UK is the European Community, but we shall be looking at this later on. Other important institutions include:

- the International Monetary Fund (IMF)
- the General Agreement on Tariffs and Trade (GATT)
- the International Bank for Reconstruction and Development ('World Bank')
- the Organisation of Petroleum Exporting Countries (OPEC).

The British sometimes find it hard to understand why we need to get mixed up with all these foreigners. The main point of most international organisations is to encourage trade. We have already seen how trade benefits the world economy.

The International Monetary Fund

The International Monetary Fund (IMF) was established in principle by the Bretton Woods Agreement in 1944 and came into being in 1947. Most of the world's countries were members. Each country had to contribute a 'quota' into the fund, 25% of it in gold and the rest in its own currency. This created a fund which was used to help member countries pay for balance of payments difficulties. There was also a system of **fixed exchange rates**. We have seen how Governments could intervene to manipulate the exchange rate of their currency. Under the Bretton Woods system, every country had to ensure that its exchange rate against other currencies did not change by more than one per cent either side of an agreed rate. The stability arising from fixed exchange rates enabled the world to enjoy a period of unprecedented growth in trade and prosperity, which lasted until the early 1970s. Some readers may be old enough to remember the swinging sixties, for instance. We *must* have been well off, considering the amount of raw material wasted on flared trouser legs and platform shoes.

By then, the Bretton Woods system was under enormous strain because of differences in inflation rates between one country and another, and the rises in oil prices. Matters were made worse by America's huge balance of payments deficit, which mounted as the war in Vietnam sucked in imports of materials. These problems created huge imbalances in payments which the system could not cope with. There just wasn't enough money in the IMF to cover every country's balance of payments debts. We have seen that a deficit country's currency shows an excess of supply over demand in exchange markets, driving the price or exchange rate down. The downward pressures on some exchange rates were so strong by the 1970s that even the funds available at the IMF were not enough to maintain fixed exchange rates. Economic forces in the currency markets overcame official attempts to fix exchange rates; finally the fixed exchange rate system had to be abandoned (though briefly revived from 1971–73).

Since then, exchange rates have been allowed to **float**, though Governments are supposed to intervene to stop any very dramatic movements. This is called 'dirty floating'. The IMF continues to oversee the system and to provide some credit facilities, including the **Special Drawing Right** (SDR), an entitlement to draw credit from the IMF. The SDR itself can be used as payment between member countries without first having to be 'cashed' at the IMF.

The General Agreement on Tariffs and Trade

The General Agreement on Tariffs and Trade (GATT) was established in 1947 and is based in Geneva. The object of the organisation is to encourage free trade and to discourage any barriers to trade, especially tariffs. Remember, economic growth means having as much trade as possible. Members, which again include most countries, are pledged not to create new barriers to trade and gradually to remove existing ones.

Every few years the members meet to try to agree reductions in tariffs and other obstacles to free trade. Current GATT negotiations are taking place in Uruguay in South America. Previous ones, for instance in Tokyo (1979–84), have led to substantial reductions in tariffs. However, because GATT has always been a compromise, there are certain loopholes. Countries can impose duties on imports if the imports were subsidised, for instance. Also, GATT only has a very small secretariat and cannot monitor all the trade policies of member countries. In addition, various more subtle forms of trade barrier have emerged in the 1980s. These range from the UK's 'voluntary' export restraint agreement with Japanese car producers to the paperwork at Greek Customs, which can easily take days or even weeks to clear up (assuming, of course, that the customs officer turns up).

The World Bank

The International Bank for Reconstruction and Development (IBRD), also known as the World Bank, was originally devised at Bretton Woods and set up in 1946. It was intended to finance post-war reconstruction, and development projects in less developed countries (LDCs). Nowadays it concentrates on the latter. It will make loans to cover part of the cost of specific projects, such as the Volta Dam and hydro-electric plant in Ghana, but also channels private funds into these projects. Funds for IBRD were originally provided by the wealthier members of the Bretton Woods agreement, such as the USA, though there is also money from loan repayments. The proportion of private funds has risen substantially over the years. Each project is carefully inspected. The interest rates are very low. The World Bank is one of several agencies which provides aid for LDCs, accounting for 42% of all aid. Others include the **United Nations**, the **European Investment Bank** (a European Community version of the World Bank) and the **Development Assistance Committee** (the 17 most prosperous industrial nations). We could perhaps do better by removing the trade barriers which currently prevent LDCs from selling goods to us, and which ensure that they remain poor.

The World Bank, the IMF and the other international agencies together could provide only a fraction of the loans needed by LDCs when oil prices rose in the 1970s; the LDCs faced huge bills for imports of oil which they could not afford. Instead, they turned in desperation to commercial banks in the West. The result of these massive loans and the crippling interest payments was a **debt crisis**. LDCs found that almost all their exports were needed to pay off interest on debt, while Western banks found that repayments were not being made. Some debt has now been painfully written off by the banks, some has been re-negotiated, and some LDCs have simply refused to pay. The problem of LDC debt persists and no long term solution has yet been found. The shareholders of Western banks wonder why their money was lent to South American dictators in the first place. Aside from dubious reputations, their tenure of office was short and their countries were poor. (How do you get your money back: invade them?) Meanwhile the LDCs wonder how they can ever improve their standard of living with all these debts to pay off. Perhaps international agencies like the IMF and World Bank should do more, or perhaps Western Governments should come up with more money.

OPEC

The Organisation of Petroleum Exporting Countries (OPEC) is a club of oil producers (mainly Middle-Eastern LDCs). Its main aim is to keep oil prices artificially high. This is done by setting a maximum output for each member to ensure a permanent slight shortage of supply. This keeps the price in the market up. Each member agrees not to try to undercut the other members. Such a price fixing agreement is called a **cartel**. OPEC twice succeeded in forcing up oil prices, with a massive four-fold increase in 1973 and a further doubling in 1979. Since the early 1980s, oil prices have tended to fall again, however. This was partly due to the Gulf War: Iran and Iraq both needed oil revenue badly, so they were prepared to over-produce and undercut other members to get as much oil revenue as possible. The result was a glut of oil and a dramatic fall in the price.

Oil prices which had been only a few dollars per barrel in the 1960s rose to $33 per barrel in 1979, but plummeted to $11 per barrel in 1985. At the time of writing, prices had recovered a little to around $18, following new OPEC agreements and the end of the Gulf War. Changes in oil prices have a dramatic impact on the world economy. Rising oil prices increase the cost of energy, and therefore put up the prices of all manufactured products. This leads to inflation in the West. The increased prices and Government measures to restrain inflation (by cutting back on consumer demand through higher taxes and/or lower Government spending) cause unemployment in the West as well. The problems of financing balance of payments deficits caused by costly oil imports also led to the breakdown of the international fixed exchange rate system and massive debts for non-OPEC LDCs. The fall in the oil price eased all these problems in the 1980s but the world is still suffering the after effects of the 1970s with high unemployment and LDC debt.

Discussion points

1. How important are international organisations?
2. Should countries give up their individual controls on trade?
3. How can we help underdeveloped countries without harming ourselves?

THE EUROPEAN COMMUNITIES

We have discussed the advantages of having more trade, how the world economy gains from the competition, specialisation and economies of scale which trade brings. The European Community is designed first and foremost to promote trade between European countries, to get these benefits. It is not necessarily intended to create a *political* union of European countries, though that could turn out to be a major side effect.

How the European Community is organised

The European Community is really a set of European Communities (the Coal and Steel Community, the Atomic Energy Commission and the European Economic Community), begun in the 1950s and then merged. The Communities are run by special international institutions. The Council of Ministers, a collection of ministers from existing national Governments, has the ultimate power. There is one minister from each country at meetings, but the voting is 'qualified' in proportion to the size of the country. Day to day the EC is run by the European Commission. There are two commissioners from each of the large countries (UK, France, Germany, Italy and Spain) and one from each of the small countries. The European Parliament has only consultative powers, though it can veto the budget. There are 518 MEPs altogether, 81 from the UK. These are directly elected by ordinary people, and countries are allocated a share of the seats in proportion to their population.

The original six member countries were France, West Germany, Italy, the Netherlands, Belgium and Luxembourg. They were joined in 1973 by the UK, Ireland and Denmark. Greece joined in 1981, and Spain and Portugal in 1986. The important characteristics of the member countries are shown below:

Population in 1987

Belgium	9.9m
Denmark	5.1m
Germany	61.1m
Greece	10.0m
France	55.6m
Ireland	3.5m
Italy	57.3m
Luxembourg	0.4m
Netherlands	14.7m
UK	56.9m
Spain	38.8m
Portugal	10.4m
EC TOTAL	323.7m

GDP in billions (thousand millions), 1987

Belgium	£78.2bn
Denmark	£54.3bn
Germany	£602.5bn
Greece	£28.2bn
France	£457.0bn
Ireland	£14.0bn
Italy	£346.1bn
Luxembourg	£4.0bn
Netherlands	£117.3bn
UK	£364.0bn
Spain	£153.8bn
Portugal	£19.8bn
Total	£2,239.8bn

Activities of the European Community

The main aim of the EC is to encourage trade between members, but it does other things as well, mainly to do with agriculture and regional aid. To finance its policies in these areas the Community has to collect money. Its own budget amounts to nearly £30 billion per year. The money is raised from a **Common External Tariff** on goods imported from non-members, by taking a small fraction of VAT revenues from member Governments and also by means of a contribution based on GDP. There is a **Regional and Social Fund**, amounting to nearly 20% of the budget, which provides money for regional and social aid. Money is given to members to spend on their own regional aid policies and the EC also helps specific social projects.

However, 63% of the money is spent on farming. Originally, the farmers were the poorest people in the Community so there was a case for helping them. Farming needs to be subsidised anyway, otherwise small farms would go out of business in a bad year. People would leave the land and go off to do other things (in my case, to become an economics teacher). Gradually, there would be fewer and fewer farms, until one day we wouldn't have enough to eat. It follows that we all stand to gain from aid to farmers. The **Common Agricultural Policy** (CAP) works by buying up huge amounts of all kinds of food (intervention buying). This pushes the price up in the market, which makes farmers better off, but also encourages over-production. It is all immensely expensive because of the need to buy and then store the produce; we end up with 'butter mountains' and 'wine lakes'. On the other hand, some kind of farm support is needed to make sure we have adequate food supplies. The answer probably lies in lower target prices and less intervention buying. Recently limits have been placed on intervention buying for beef, and production quotas (limiting farm production) have been established for cereals and milk.

The European Monetary System (EMS)

In its efforts to promote more trade, the Community met a serious obstacle; the problem throughout the 1970s was **currency instability**. Suppose a French company wants to sell pens in the UK and British people will pay £1 for a pen. Let's say that £1 = F10 and that F10 is just enough to make production profitable. By the time the French company has started production and got the pens to the UK, the exchange rate might have changed. If the exchange rate moves to £ = F8 the French pen manufacturer gets 2F less than expected for each pen. This might mean a loss. If they increase the price of the pen say to £1.20, it might be much harder to sell if there are cheaper ones available. This risk of loss through sudden changes in exchange rates poses a serious threat to trade. In many cases firms just wouldn't bother to try to trade because of this risk.

To combat this risk, the **European Monetary System** (EMS) was established in 1979. Members of the EC fixed the value of their currencies against each other. The exchange rate between any pair of currencies was to be kept within a band of 2.25% either side of an agreed rate. Italy was allowed a 6% margin for the volatile lira, though this was narrowed to 2.25% in January 1990. The UK decided not to fix the sterling exchange rate at all. Greece also declined to fix its exchange rate when it joined, as did Portugal. Spain brought the peseta into the system within a 6% band in June 1989.

To fix the value of their exchange rates, Governments must intervene in the exchange markets to buy and sell their currencies (extra buying and selling can be used to manipulate the price). Extra reserves were provided to help with this by setting up a European Monetary Co-operation Fund (EMCF). Each member deposited 20% of its reserves of foreign currency into the Fund; in return, the Fund gave them an equivalent amount in **European Currency Units** (ECU), which it simply printed. Governments agreed to accept ECU in payments between themselves and this had the effect of increasing effective reserves.

The ECU is a curious species. It is a kind of 'hybrid', being made up of bits of other currencies which are stuck together. Sterling and the drachma are included in the ECU even though they are not part of the fixed exchange rate system. One ECU is made up as follows:

ECU1 = £0.09 + DM0.6 + FF1.3 + Gu0.22 + BF3.3 + LuxF0.14
      + Li151 + Kr0.20 + Ir£0.009 + Dr1.1 + Pe6.9 + Es1.4

The amounts of each currency in this 'basket' were originally calculated to make ECU1 the same as $1. Each currency has a certain 'weight' in the basket according to that country's share of European trade. Nearly a third of the value of the ECU is accounted for by the DM0.6 of the Germans. The weights also work out so that about half the value of the ECU is made up of strong currencies (DM, Danish Kroner, Dutch Guilder) and the rest of weak currencies. This makes the overall value of the ECU very stable, measured in terms of any outside currency, such as dollars or Yen.

Originally, the ECU was just a means of payment between Governments. No ECUs were issued to the public. However, because it is so stable the ECU has become widely used in private business, even though there are no ECU banknotes in existence. Private individuals can use the ECU as a unit of account. Many Italian imports are invoiced in ECUs. Invoicing in the volatile Lira would mean that the value of the payment could vary quite significantly between the time when the invoice is sent and the time when the money is received (also, there might not be enough room on the invoice for all the zeros needed when you use Lira). ECU is now one of the most popular denominations for international bonds (IOUs). If someone issues a seven year bond, then the value of the loan could change during the seven years if it is fixed in, say, £ or $. To avoid this problem, we can fix the value of the loan in ECUs, which are much more stable.

Because of the growing popularity of the ECU in private business, eighteen European banks set up an ECU clearing system in 1985. The **Mutual ECU Settlement Account** (MESA) lets people hold bank accounts in ECU, and write cheques to each other in ECU, without having to change their money back into national currencies. Of course, depositing money into the account to start with, or cashing cheques, must involve national currencies, since there is no cash in the form of ECUs. Over five hundred other banks worldwide also deal in ECUs. It may be that a common European currency has arrived by stealth.

The Common Market

The original vision of the Community was to create a single integrated market throughout Europe, without any barriers to trade. Member countries could then enjoy all the benefits of extra competition, specialisation and economies of scale discussed earlier. It would be easier to compete with large American and Japanese firms, both at home and abroad, and this would bring even more benefits. When the Community was first set up all tariffs and other more obvious barriers to trade were removed. The obstacles to trade from currency instability had largely been removed in 1979 by the creation of the EMS. However, there remained other important, less visible, barriers to free trade within the EC. The result was that, instead of having a single integrated European market, we had twelve small national markets, between which trade was still difficult. In 1986 agreement was reached on a series of measures to remove the remaining barriers, visible and invisible, to create a genuine common market by the end of 1992.

By 1992, **border controls** will be abolished. At present, delays to lorries moving goods across national borders create a serious obstacle to trade. Because of bureaucratic paperwork, lorries can be held up for two or three days. This creates a lot of expense for traders; they have to pay the drivers, and they need extra lorries; they also need more stocks, both at the production end and the distribution end. Total costs to industry of border delays are estimated at £8 billion per year, and in the end customers have to meet this bill through higher prices.

Another major obstacle to free trade is differing **safety standards** in each country. This is a headache for all manufacturing industries. For example, in some countries cars must not have asbestos brake linings, in others they must have yellow headlights, in others special mirrors. All these modifications are expensive and make it impossible to benefit fully from economies of scale. Costs are therefore higher than they need be. If we take the French firm Peugeot as an example, these extra costs are estimated to be £200m per year for this one company. By 1992 there will be a common set of standards, so that firms will only have to manufacture one version of their product rather than twelve slightly different ones.

The **role of Governments** will also have to be modified. At the moment when Governments buy things for themselves, like police cars or hospitals, they usually only buy from firms in their own country. This means that firms operating in areas where Governments do most of the spending cannot enjoy free trade in a large

European market, but are restricted to their smaller national market. After 1992, Governments will be obliged to offer their contracts to firms throughout the Community. It will also be against the rules for Governments to subsidise their industries by giving them cash handouts, since this would give them an unfair advantage. If we are to get the benefits of free competition throughout Europe, firms must not be artificially cushioned in this competitive struggle. Governments will also have to harmonise the various taxes they impose on things like alcohol, cigarettes and petrol. If they continue to charge widely differing rates, as at present, they will find it difficult to collect the taxes. Suppose wine carries a £2 tax in the UK and none in France, then everyone will buy from France, and after 1992 there won't be any customs controls to collect the extra tax when people bring the wine back.

A fully integrated single market will also have to allow totally free movement of labour and capital throughout the Community. This may pose a few problems if all the Greeks decide to move to Germany, or all the British to Spain, but language and cultural barriers should prevent too much of this. The main problem with free movements of capital is that massive flows of currency from one country to another will make it very difficult to maintain the fixed exchange rates in the EMS (selling and buying currencies causes changes in the market price, the exchange rate).

Although a Europe without barriers may seem a bit strange, one has only to consider the notion of barriers *within* countries to see how sensible it is. Imagine having to stop on your way from London to Birmingham to declare whether you had any alcohol. Imagine not being able to apply for a job in Liverpool if you lived in Manchester. Imagine having to swap Yorkshire £ for Sussex £ when you go down to Brighton for the day. Ridiculous? Then why put up with those same obstacles between Britain and France, or between Germany and Italy? The prospect of 1992 is already overturning age-old traditions. The British now talk about learning foreign languages, the French are considering putting a tax on wine, and rumours from Athens suggest that the Greeks may finally have discovered timetables.

The prospects for Europe

The prospect now is for the eventual creation of a single integrated common market in Europe. However, the different currencies will still remain. Although exchange rates are now stable under the EMS, not all countries are participating fully in the EMS. In any case, a truly integrated European economy would have the same currency. In 1988, the French and Italians proposed the creation of a European Central Bank, which would eventually control European money and replace national currencies with an EC currency. In early 1989, a committee of central bankers under the chairmanship of M Delors, President of the EC Commission, produced a report proposing a three-stage process to complete monetary union. The first phase involves full membership of the EMS for the remaining currencies still outside. Phase two would consist of setting up a European Central Bank. The third and final phase would be the adoption of a new European currency. Mrs Thatcher is dragging her heels. The problem is that one currency means one economic policy. This implies very close political co-operation, if not political union. It certainly transfers the most important policy-making powers from national Governments to the EC. Talk of EC-wide 'social policies' also frightens the Conservative British Premier. However, with the private use of the ECU increasing, and the difficulties of trade in different currencies highlighted after 1992, the pressure for a common currency has led the other eleven countries to accept the Delors Report. If Mrs Thatcher persists in her opposition, the others may go ahead without the UK, leaving us outside the single currency zone and making our trade with Europe more risky and expensive than need be.

Other future developments might involve the enlargement of the EC to include more countries. Non-members who trade heavily with the Community will find themselves having to obey the EC rules on common standards and so on. Non-members, of course, have no say in setting these common standards, which means that they actually have *less* say in their own affairs than members. Far from having more sovereignty, non-members will end up with less. For this reason Austria and Cyprus have applied for membership and will probably join in the 1990s. Norway might apply, but the Norwegians voted to stay out in 1972, so it may be difficult for the Norwegian Government to persuade its population. Sweden and Switzerland are supposed to be neutral and so membership of a Western club may be politically difficult for them. Turkey and Morocco have applied to join but are unlikely to be accepted in the near future because their economies are so underdeveloped. It would be difficult to integrate an underdeveloped country because they won't be rich enough to buy much from other members and their industries won't be efficient enough to compete for trade in other countries. Eastern European countries, which have started to become democracies with free markets, may also wish to join eventually.

Discussion points

1. Do the economic benefits of single European economy outweigh the loss of political sovereignty?
2. Should it be as easy to trade with Paris as it is to trade between London and Liverpool?
3. Should we have a single currency?
4. Should depressed areas like Liverpool introduce their own currency and devalue it against the British pound to encourage trade?

6

The Government and the Economy

GOVERNMENT INDUSTRIAL POLICY

The Government can use various industrial policies to try to make the economy work better. For example it can encourage enterprise, so that more people start up new businesses. It can try to foster improved efficiency through more competition. This will make firms more successful, giving the consumer a better deal and employing more people. It can get involved in industry directly by means of nationalised industries. A final possibility is to encourage the labour force to become more suited to industry's needs.

New enterprise

The importance of new enterprise in an economy cannot be exaggerated. The level of economic activity depends crucially on the number of enterprises. When a firm is set up it employs at least one person (the person starting the business) and usually several more. New firms also produce goods and services. If they succeed it is because people want to buy their goods and services. This means that consumers benefit as well as employees. The real problem is: how can we encourage more people to become entrepreneurs?

Perhaps the biggest change in the economy during the Thatcher years in the 1980s is the creation of what has become known as the 'enterprise culture'. This is in stark contrast to previous attitudes. Before 1979, 'business' was often a dirty word. People in business were regarded as self-seeking parasites, exploiting workers and consumers for personal profit. Now they are seen as self-reliant, providing jobs and prosperity for the benefit of all. The pre-Thatcher view of business, often based on envy, or out-of-date social attitudes, resulted in a prejudice against commerce throughout society. This had the effect of discouraging young people from going into business. Teachers (who had all opted for the 'professions' by definition) encouraged bright youngsters to become doctors, solicitors and accountants; we seldom got our best people into the large industrial companies or setting up their own firms.

In a concerted and prolonged propoganda war, the Conservatives have virtually reversed these attitudes to create a pro-business, 'yuppie' society. Equally important is the Government's insistence that people must stand on their own two feet. In the 1980s the Government refused to bail out sinking industries ('lame ducks'). This meant that many companies whose products were no longer in demand, or which faced cheaper competition from abroad, went under. In the mass unemployment that followed, people often had little choice but to start up their own business. In many cases, redundancy pay from their previous firm, amounting to many thousands of pounds, was available as capital.

The Government also has policies directly designed to help new enterprise get off the ground. There are three main strands to these policies. The first concerns making it easier for small firms to raise the capital they need to get going.

- The **Business Expansion Scheme** (BES) offers tax relief for people who put money into small businesses.
- The **Loan Guarantee Scheme** guarantees borrowing for entrepreneurs who can't put up security (eg a house) to obtain a loan.
- The **Unlisted Securities Market** (USM) was introduced on the Stock Exchange to make it possible to buy and sell shares in small companies.

A second Government approach has involved tax allowances and grants to small businesses. Corporation tax was cut from over 50% to 35%, with a special rate for small firms of 25%. There is also an **Enterprise Allowance Scheme** which gives unemployed people who set up a business £40 per week to help with living expenses.

The third type of action was in the area of Government interference. The Conservatives have sought to free small businesses from 'hassles' resulting from Government regulations and controls. For example, small firms are now exempt from certain rules relating to unfair dismissals, and there is help in dealing with rates and VAT.

Government assistance

The Thatcher Government is reluctant to provide state aid to industry; it believes that firms will not become efficient and com-

petitive if they can rely on the Government to rescue them. If firms
are faced with the stark choice of either improving their performance or going under, then both management and workers will try
harder to succeed. There is also an economic argument for allowing unprofitable firms to fail. A company may often become
unprofitable because people no longer want its products (slide
rules, for instance). Trying to keep production going in these
circumstances is merely a waste of resources which could be used
to make things people *do* want to buy. The Conservatives' views
on Government assistance are highlighted by their policy—or
rather lack of policy—on regional development. Traditionally,
Governments tried to lure manufacturing firms from the prosperous South East to the North by various automatic grants. These
grants have been reduced by redefining the 'depressed regions' to
cover a much smaller area, and by making the grants available at
the discretion of the Government rather than automatically.

Competition policy

Government policy has always emphasised the importance of having several firms in the market for a particular product. When
firms compete for customers, they are forced to charge lower
prices and offer a better service. The quality of the meat in
Stavros' kebabs may suddenly improve if Costas sets up a rival
take-away just down the road, and Stavros' prices will probably
fall. The customer obviously benefits from this. In order to offer a
lower price, firms also need to cut their costs; in other words they
must become more efficient. Improving efficiency may mean
installing the latest machinery, or having more flexible working
practices, or simply working harder. People tend to resist all this,
but in the end it is absolutely essential. If British firms are not
efficient and their costs are higher than those of their Japanese
competitors, they will simply lose their customers and go out of
business.

Some Government-owned industries used to have a legal monopoly: it was illegal for anyone else to compete with them. British
Telecom was one example, until the Government changed the law
to allow Mercury into the market. This kind of barrier to competition is rare, however. The main threat to healthy competition is
the merger of firms. When firms combine there are fewer firms in
the market. Lots of mergers ultimately lead to less competition.
Mergers can either involve two firms uniting or one firm taking
over another by buying 51% or more of its shares. Because of the
threat to competition, the Government may investigate mergers

which involve more than 25% of the market share or more than £15 million of assets. It does this by referring the takeover or merger to the **Monopolies and Mergers Commission** (MMC), a body of impartial experts. The Commission may decide that a merger is against the public interest, in which case it may be barred. Several big takeover bids were referred to the Commission in the late 1980s. A proposed merger between the electrical giants GEC and Plessey in 1986 was blocked; GEC and the German company, Siemens, launched another bid for Plessey in 1989. A bid by Minorco for Consolidated Goldfields was eventually cleared, but the delay damaged Minorco's position and ConsGold eventually went instead to Hanson for £3.5bn.

But not all mergers are against the public interest:

- Mergers may for example lead to **economies of scale** (which reduce unit costs) in some industries. This was true in the car industry in the 1960s and 1970s.

- More mergers are needed soon so that larger firms with more economies of scale can take advantage of the large **integrated European market** after 1992.

Takeover bids also help to keep management on its toes. A badly run company will make low profits, and thus low dividend payments to shareholders. The shareholders will start selling their shares if this happens. Widespread selling of a company's shares leads to a fall in the share price. Once the share price is low enough, someone else is likely to consider the firm a good bargain and launch a bid to buy up its shares and take it over. A new owner will probably get rid of existing senior management and the only way to avoid this is to keep the share price up by making the company profitable. For these reasons, the Government will not refer many mergers to the MMC and the MMC may clear some that are referred.

Nationalisation and privatisation
The Government's direct involvement in the economy takes the form of **nationalised industries**. A nationalised industry is one owned entirely by the Government. These industries were originally set up by Labour after the war to give ownership of the 'commanding heights of the economy' to ordinary people. The problem was that Governments used the nationalised industries as a tool of policy: if transport services were needed in remote areas,

then British Rail was told to provide them; if the Government was trying to keep inflation down, the nationalised industries weren't allowed to put their prices up; if the Government was short of money, nationalised industries were kept short of funds to invest or modernise. Such interference made it difficult for the nationalised industries to be profitable. Things were made worse by the fact that most of them were monopolies. Also, everyone knew a nationalised industry could never go bankrupt. A nationalised industry is part of the Government and the Government is never bankrupt. The management and unions in these safe monopolies therefore had little incentive to become more efficient; the result was poor quality of service and high costs leading to huge losses. The losses at British Steel were measured in millions of pounds *per day*, or thousands of pounds per minute.

The Thatcher Government has pursued a policy of **privatisation**, the opposite of nationalisation. The nationalised industries now account for only 5% of GDP, as compared with 10% in the 1970s. The idea is to sell off the nationalised industries and put them back into the private sector. This cuts out Government interference and allows the industries to be run efficiently, borrowing money for investment where necessary and charging commercial prices. Privatisation was accompanied in some cases by new competition, as with BT and Mercury, though Mercury is too small to compete effectively with BT. Competition and the profit motive, together with the threat of bankruptcy in the event of failure, ought to create more incentives for both management and unions to be efficient.

It should be pointed out, however, that all this *could* be achieved without any transfer of ownership. In order for anyone to want shares in the nationalised industries, they first had to be made profitable; if they can be made profitable while still under Government control, then why can't they *always* be profitable under Government control? Surely all the Government has to do is to behave like private shareholders and sack the management, or close plants, when the industry is inefficient?

In practice the nationalised monopolies have also tended to become private monopolies without any real competition. Partly this is because some industries are 'natural monopolies', where economies of scale are so important that there should only be one firm. Another reason, however, is that shares in a profitable monopoly are more attractive and therefore easier for the Government to sell off. Much of the reasoning behind privatisation seems to be political. It was a good way of getting millions of people involved in owning shares. Share ownership, by a strange coincidence, goes hand in hand with voting Conservative. Widespread share ownership, or 'popular capitalism' as Mrs Thatcher calls it, seems to be one way of ensuring that large industries are owned by the general public. It has the advantage of giving (some) members of the public more direct ownership than they had when industries were owned on their behalf by the Government.

Performance of privatised companies
Sales per worker

British Aerospace	1981	£26,700;	1987	£41,600
British Telecom	1984	£32,100;	1987	£40,000
Jaguar	1984	£65,600;	1987	£73,300
Cable & Wireless	1981	£33,000;	1987	£35,700
Britoil	1983	£472,000;	1987	£412,000

(oil price collapse in 1985)

Government labour policies

A persistent problem in the UK economy has been the mismatch between the skills of workers and the skills required by industries. Even with millions unemployed, some industries have still been unable to fill job vacancies because applicants lack the right qualifications. This problem has led to a rash of training schemes:

- For school leavers there is the **Youth Training Scheme** (where the Government pays for a year or two of work experience).
- For adults there is **Employment Training** for the long term unemployed.

The blame for this problem must, however, ultimately rest with our education system. We have tended to try to give everyone an 'academic' sort of education, based heavily on books. Many children are not much interested in reading and thinking; they like *doing* things. It is precisely the practical skills youngsters enjoy which the economy needs. The new **GCSE** examination is supposed to be more practical, and there are moves to create more practical education through the **Certificate of Pre-Vocational Education** (CPVE) and the **Training and Vocational Education Initiative** (TVEI).

The Government has also sought to make the labour market more responsive to industry's needs by limiting the power of **trade unions**. Trade unions can create inefficiency in firms in two ways. Firstly, they can raise the wage rate, which means that the cost per unit of output is higher. Secondly, they can resist the introduction of new (labour saving) technology, which also means that costs per unit will be higher than necessary. The result is that British companies may find it difficult to compete with foreigners. The Thatcher Government passed a series of measures to make strike action more difficult, by outlawing sympathy strikes and strikes without ballots. These measures, together with unemployment, which reduced union membership and made workers reluctant to risk strikes, have weakened the unions. Major victories have been won by managements seeking to introduce more efficient practices into industry. Examples include the rationalisation of British Steel (1980), the pit closures by the National Coal Board (1985) and the abolition of the National Dock Labour Scheme (1989).

These 'confrontation policies' seem to have worked rather better in reshaping industrial activity than the 'consensus politics' that went before. Previous Governments tried to reach voluntary agreements with unions to limit pay increases, encouraging more productivity where possible. Pay controls were tried frequently throughout the 1960s and 1970s; they limited wage rises for a while, but in the end they all broke down and were followed by periods of rapidly rising incomes, and accelerating inflation. In other countries, such as Japan and West Germany, unions and management had worked together for industrial efficiency, without the sort of hostility common in the UK until the 1980s. It remains to be seen whether the Thatcher era has permanently changed trade union behaviour, however. An upsurge of strikes in 1989 raises doubts over this question.

Discussion points
1. Has Thatcherism reshaped the British industrial landscape?
2. Why were unions striking again in 1989–90?
3. Should mergers be more tightly controlled?
4. Has privatisation now gone too far?

GOVERNMENT SPENDING AND TAXATION POLICIES

Governments in all modern societies spend money to provide various services. The Government also raises money through the different taxes it imposes on its citizens. Both the provision of services, and the imposition of taxes, affect the economy of a country. The link between Government spending and taxation is also important. The Government need not balance its spending and its income any more than individuals need to. The way in which any financial surplus or deficit is dealt with will also affect the economy.

How Government developed

Government was primarily designed in the past to control and provide security for the state. The main function of the British Government was to impose the will of the monarch and, later, to ensure law and order under a constitutionally elected Prime Minister and Cabinet. Money was needed to provide both internal and external defence forces for the state. The rulers had to keep their own people in line (in case they had any dangerous ideas about freedom or equality); and on the other hand they had to fend off foreign threats, from the Spanish, French and Germans, for example. A police force emerged in the mid-nineteenth century; armies had been paid for by the Government to defend the nation for centuries before that. The creation of the British Empire and the threat from Napoleon, and later on the Germans, led to big rises in the fraction of the country's income that had to be spent in this way.

By the early 1900s, however, people began to demand another form of security from the Government—**social security**. Some people had the curious notion that everyone was entitled to a decent living, even if they were sick or old or out of work. The Liberal Government of 1906 began the process which finally led to the modern **Welfare State**: the idea of National Insurance was born. People were to pay contributions, and in return receive sickness benefits, unemployment benefits and pensions. By 1948, under Attlee's Labour Government, the Welfare State had expanded to include free medical services, low rent Government housing (through local councils) and social workers. The idea of Governments looking after the people became widely accepted; and it was the opposite view which now seemed outrageous.

There was more to come. The Labour Party's constitution committed it in clause 4 to the 'Common Ownership of the Means of Production'. In other words, we should all own the main industries, instead of a few rich capitalists owning everything; the Government should actually own and run industries on behalf of society. From 1945 onwards an extensive range of industries was nationalised (bought from the owners), including all the main **public utilities**, such as rail, telephones, gas and electricity, and other important activities, such as steel, airways and car manufacturing. This historic trend has now been firmly reversed by the

Thatcher Government, with the privatisation of many industries (selling them back to private shareholders).

Public expenditure in the UK

Government spending is called **public expenditure**. Total public expenditure in 1988–9 was over £150bn or about 40% of the national income. The big four areas for spending were as follows:

Social Security payments:	£47bn	(28%)
(falling as unemployment drops)		
Health and personal social services:	£22bn	(14%)
Education and science:	£19bn	(12%)
Defence:	£19bn	(12%)

Between them, these four items account for more than 60% of all Government spending. Most other activities account for just a few per cent each, except for large **interest payments** on past debt. Interest paid by the Government in 1988 was £17bn, making total public expenditure including interest of around £170bn. The interest burden is falling, however, because the Government is now repaying large amounts of past debt.

Most people accept the need for public services such as defence, schools, hospitals, roads and so on. They are also the sort of thing that individuals can hardly organise for themselves (in the past children from poor families just didn't go to school). The balance between the various sorts of spending is largely a matter for political debate. Should we spend less on nuclear weapons? Should we spend more on health or education? Such issues all depend on personal opinion and there can be no scientific answer. One thing is sure, however: we cannot spend more of *everything*. To build more hospitals may mean less money for schools; more roads may mean less defence, and so on. If public expenditure as a whole rises, there will be less left over for private consumption. It's just the same for a teenager with £5 of his pocket money left to spend; he can either afford two doner kebabs for himself and his girlfriend, or a Bros record for himself, but he can't afford both (so he buys the kebabs). The size of the financial cake is limited; if one slice gets larger, other slices must get smaller. The problem, as always, is that there is a strong case for increasing the size of almost every slice (particularly health and education in the late 1980s), which is impossible.

Some people have gone further and argued that the fraction of the national cake taken by the Government actually tends to make the cake itself smaller. Why should this be? There are two main lines of argument:

- The first is that private industry is the productive sector of the economy. If the Government buys up land, machinery and labour for things like social services, there will be **fewer resources** left over for productive private industries that actually manufacture goods. The private economy will therefore not be as productive as it could be, and we may not be able to sell enough exports to pay for all our imports.

- The other argument is that where industries are nationalised they tend to be **less efficient**. There is little incentive for nationalised industries to be efficient because there is no profit motive or threat of bankruptcy. A lack of efficiency makes it even harder to export and compete against foreign imports.

The end result is **de-industrialisation**, or fewer and fewer jobs in manufacturing. If we can reduce the fraction of the economy in the public sector we should get more of it devoted to productive private sector manufacturing industry, and there should be more efficiency within that industry. We should then be able to restore our exports and competitiveness and have a successful industrial sector employing more people.

The evidence on all this is inconclusive, however. There is no obvious shortage of resources, at the moment. In France, state owned industries have tended to operate more profitably. Also, the UK Government seems to have no difficulty making nationalised industries 'profitable' in order to sell them off. Why can't it keep them profitable? Extending the efficiency arguments to the Government services themselves, the Conservatives are trying to bring in a more competitive, business-minded approach in health and education to improve the quality of services without actually spending more money (which we don't have). The proposed reforms have led to heated debate from people who argue that the quality of services will inevitably suffer if too much emphasis is placed on financial efficiency.

The fact that public expenditure looms so large in the national economy is quite useful in another way. It means that the Government is able to influence the economy quite dramatically. It can use public expenditure to affect the economy both directly and indirectly. For example, money spent by the Government on services like education and the police creates a direct demand, for police cars, textbooks, teachers, and so on. Money given as hand-outs to the unemployed or poor people is spent and this also creates an indirect demand for goods and services in the economy. Both direct and indirect effects can lead to more output and more jobs in the economy. We have heard the argument, however, that things may be better in the long run without too much Government activity.

Taxation in the UK

The Government imposes various forms of taxation to pay for all the public expenditure we have been talking about. We don't normally expect to get something without paying for it. The argument that too much Government interference damages the economy applies to taxation as well. Conservatives argue that high rates of tax discourage people from working hard and from starting up businesses. High personal taxes may also create a 'brain drain' as well qualified people go to work abroad where taxes are lower. The cuts in UK tax rates since 1979 seem to have increased business success, but the evidence is not conclusive. Many other factors have contributed to the enterprise boom, and we cannot

'Next year, pay the taxes before you buy the car, darling!'

prove which was the most important. International evidence shows that the effects of high and low taxes on economic activity are variable and unpredictable.

There are other arguments against cutting taxes:

- Taxes generally take more from the rich, and the public services they pay for benefit mainly the poor. They therefore help to create a **'fairer' distribution of income**. The definition of the word 'fair' is, of course, open to interpretation and this generates heated debate, as has been discussed earlier.

- Cutting taxes puts money back into the hands of consumers, leading to an increase in total spending. The **extra demand** in the economy can then cause inflation. This was one of the criticisms of the Lawson Budget in 1988, when income tax was substantially reduced.

The most obvious taxes are the **personal taxes**. Personal taxes include:

income tax
national insurance contributions
capital gains
inheritance tax.

Income Tax (see chapter 7) is a tax on income from employment. You are allowed a certain amount of tax-free income and the rest is then taxed at 25% (1990). For income above a certain level the tax is 40% though the first chunk is still taxed at only 25%. **National insurance contributions** range from zero for the very poor to 9% (maximum contribution £26 per week) for higher earners; it thus amounts to an extra income tax. The money is supposed to be used specifically for things like sickness benefit and unemployment benefit. **Capital gains tax** is a tax on the increase in value of property between the time it is bought and the time it is sold. This means that people who make money from buying and selling shares, for instance, can still be taxed, even though they have not earned any income from employment. **Inheritance tax** is a tax on bequests or gifts made within seven years of the giver's death.

Company taxes are another source of money. **Corporation tax** is 30% (1990) or 25% for smaller companies. There is also a special **petrol revenue tax** for North Sea oil producers, charged at 60% of their sales revenue. Apart from company taxes, various taxes are charged on the sale of goods. These sales taxes are usually passed on to the customer in the form of higher prices. There are particular taxes on things like alcohol and tobacco, called **excise duties**. The official argument for taxing alcohol and tobacco is that it makes us less likely to damage our health by consuming them. The real reason, of course, is that it brings in lots of revenue. There is also a general sales tax, **value added tax** (VAT), charged at 15% of the price on most goods.

The main earners for the Government in the 1988–9 total tax take of over £180bn were as follows:

Income tax	23%
VAT	14%
Rates	10%
Corporation tax	10%
National Insurance	17%
Other	26%
Total	100%

Government borrowing

Governments seldom have the same level of public expenditure as they do taxation. They usually spend *more* than they earn, or *less*. This is very like an individual's finances; some people end the year saving and others end the year borrowing. The Government is in the same position. If Government spends more than it receives in tax revenues, it is forced to borrow the difference. If it spends less than taxes, there is a surplus. If it spends more than it gets in taxes, there is a deficit, or **public sector borrowing requirements** (PSBR). There are two ways of financing the PSBR. The Government can sell bonds (IOUs) to people or the banks. The alternative is to print more money. If there is a budget surplus rather than a deficit, the PSBR is a negative number. The Government can use the surplus to repay past debt (of which there is plenty!), or allow money to be taken out of circulation.

Government policies on money and borrowing are referred to as **monetary policy**; the policies on Government spending and taxation are called **fiscal policy**. Clearly, the two are closely linked. The balance of Government spending and taxing (fiscal policy) has to be financed by borrowing or printing money (monetary policy). If there is a surplus because of fiscal policy, it will have to be disposed of through monetary policy.

Of course, the Government's spending and earnings decisions affect us all. If it spends more than it takes in taxes, total demand in the economy will tend to rise. Conversely, if it spends less than it takes in taxes, total demand will tend to fall. The balance between Government spending and taxation is one of the most important ways of controlling demand and so economic activity.

Throughout the 1980s, the Thatcher Government has tried to prevent total demand from rising too rapidly, because it tends to cause inflation; it has tried to curb spending, both by consumers and by itself. To help curb demand the PSBR was steadily reduced to zero, and then, in the late 1980s, a public sector surplus was generated, the first for many years. Public expenditure is being kept from rising, while tax revenues are pouring in far beyond the level needed for public expenditure. The surplus was more than £14bn in 1988–9 and at a slightly lower level in 1989–90. The effect is to take money out of consumers pockets so that they can't spend it. The Government refuses to spend it either, thus keeping the lid on total demand. Surplus revenue is being used to repay past debt. The accumulated national debt in the UK had reached more than £170bn in the 1970s, and the interest payments on this debt amount to 10% of total public expenditure. Reducing the national debt will leave scope for more tax cuts, or more public expenditure, in years to come.

Discussion points
1. Should taxes be higher or lower?
2. Is the Government spending too little on services? If so, where should the extra money come from?
3. Can you think of any new kinds of taxes or benefits to introduce?

GOVERNMENT MONETARY POLICY

You might think that controlling **money** is quite simple when the Government itself gets it printed. This is far from the truth, however. To begin with no one knows what 'money' actually is. As we shall see, 'money' is a very complex concept that cannot easily be defined. *You* try controlling something when you don't even know what it is. We do, of course, have some idea what money is, so we are not entirely lost. There are several ways of trying to keep 'money' under control, and this we summarise as **monetary policy**.

What is 'money'?
The problem with defining money arises because all sorts of things, apart from **banknotes and coins**, can be used as a medium for exchange in transactions. What about **current accounts** in banks,

which you can spend by writing a cheque? What about **credit cards** and **charge cards** which can also be 'spent', in the sense that you can buy things with them? In addition to this, money in **deposit accounts** with banks and building societies represents potential spending. Of course, you have to take it out before you can spend it (easy enough with automatic machines in the wall), but it is still important.

The point is that all these various forms of money and financial assets *can affect purchasing power*. If the Government wants to control purchasing power it must control the supply of all kinds of money, including credit and deposits. We saw earlier how total demand for goods and services in the economy helps decide levels of growth, inflation and unemployment. As the Government wants to control demand, so it must control purchasing power, and so it must control money.

Before the Government can try to control money it needs to define it. There are in fact a whole series of official definitions of money. Some of them are 'narrow' measures, which count mainly cash; others are 'broad' measures, which count various forms of credit or deposits as well as cash. The official definitions sound like motorways: M0, M1, M2, M3, M4 and M5. They get broader as the number goes up; M0, M1 and M2 represent narrow money, and M3, M4 and M5 broad money. Briefly they are as follows:

M0 = Cash with the public and in the banks.

M1 = Cash with the public + current accounts in banks.

M2 = Cash + current accounts + building society share accounts + National Savings ordinary accounts.

M3 = M1 + bank deposit accounts + bank certificates of deposit (IOUs).

M3c = M3 + foreign currency deposits in UK banks.

M4 = M3 + building society share accounts − building society holdings of bank deposits.

M5 = M4 + private sector holdings of various IOUs (eg Treasury bills, certificates of tax deposit, national savings certificates, local authority bills).

The different definitions are called **monetary aggregates**. Why do we need so many? Well, we might be interested in different forms of money for several reasons. One reason, however, is that people simply cannot agree which one to use, especially where the Government's monetary policy is concerned. There is so much

'I think I understand M-Money now, but does my pocket
money count as M0, M1, M2 or M3?'

argument over what money actually is that people need several
definitions in the hope that one of them might be the right basis. In
pursuit of one that works, the Government occasionally changes
what is counted in each of the various definitions above. We
therefore have six different aggregates, each one liable to mean
different things from time to time. As if all these definitions were
not enough, statistics are also published for things like bank lending, and some people think this figure is more important. You will
appreciate now why I said that no one knows what money actually
is.

Controlling the supply of money

Any attempt to control total demand for goods and services in the
economy clearly needs control of all purchasing power. This is
bound to mean control of both narrow *and* broad money; clearly,
both cash and bank or building society deposits will be important
in deciding the level of spending power (even if we cannot decide
exactly what counts). It is the Bank of England which operates the
Government's monetary policies; it prints cash and tries to control

deposits. Let's now look at the weapons used by the Government in its monetary policy, to control both cash and deposits.

Controlling the supply of cash money

The Government can influence the flow of cash into the economy by its own budgeting. It does so by manipulating its own spending and taxation, and therefore the level of its borrowing. Let's use the following abbreviations:

G = Government spending.
T = Taxation.
PSBR = Public Sector (Government) Borrowing Requirement.
B = Actual Government borrowing (by issuing bonds or IOUs in exchange for cash).
Ms = The supply of money (in cash form).

If the Government spends more than it gets from taxes it will have a borrowing requirement. This can be financed either by actually borrowing (issuing bonds) or by simply printing more cash. The relationship between all these can be summarised as follows:

$$G - T = PSBR = \text{Increased Ms} + B.$$

Rearranging this relationship, we get:

$$\text{Increased Ms} = G - T - B.$$

Are you confused by the mathematics? If so, just think of it like this: the increase in cash in the economy is the difference between how much the Government puts into the economy and how much it takes out. This will be equal to the amount of money spent by the Government (Government spending puts money *into* the economy); take away the amount raised in taxes (taxes take money *out of* the economy); take away Government borrowing (this also takes money *out of* the economy).

All this gives the Government three instruments with which to influence cash: Government spending, Taxation, and Government Borrowing.

- Suppose it wants to **restrict the money supply:** the Government must spend less, tax more, or borrow more (or any combination of these). Once money is taken out of circulation in this way, the Government must keep it in the Bank of England where it cannot be used.

- To **loosen the money supply** and allow more money into the system, the Government must spend more, tax less, or borrow less (or any combination of these). The Government can even repay past debts, which puts money back into the system. Repaying debt does not have the same effect, however, as increasing Government spending or reducing taxes. Tax cuts and Government spending are both likely to lead to more demand in the economy. People holding Government debt, such as Government bonds, on the other hand are savers; debt repayment therefore tends to go into savings rather than consumption and there is less risk of excessive demand. This is why the Government felt it could use its surplus revenues to repay debts in the late 1980s.

Controlling deposit money

Controlling deposit money is rather more complicated. How do bank or building society deposits affect spending? One thing which happens is that people simply take their deposits out and spend them. But, of course, on any particular day, most bank deposits are *not* required by their owners. After all, if you need to use the cash, it would be pretty stupid to put it in the bank, wouldn't it? However, the fact that most deposits are not required by their owners *means that banks can lend the money out to other people*. People borrow money from the banks in order to spend it (on hi-fi equipment, cars, holidays, etc). Most bank and building society deposits *do* therefore tend to end up as spending, either by the people who deposited the money, or by other people who borrow it from the bank or building society.

The best way to stop deposits being used for spending is to put up **interest rates**:

1. High interest rates make it harder for borrowers to borrow the deposits out of the banks and building societies, because the interest costs so much.

2. High interest rates also take money out of the pockets of people who have *already* borrowed, especially those with mortgages.

3. High interest rates encourage depositors to leave their money in the bank or building society, because they earn more by doing so. They may even put more deposits into the bank or building society than they would otherwise do.

In all these ways high interest rates mean less spending in the economy.

The Government can control interest rates by means of its own borrowing through the issue of bonds. Government bonds carry a certain interest rate, and banks are forced to offer depositors the same interest rate or people will put all their money into Government bonds. If interest on deposits goes up, then the interest charged by the banks to borrowers will also go up (to maintain the banks' profit margin). An alternative is for the Government simply to arrange with the big banks to put up their interest rates whenever it tells them to.

The Government could also try to control the *quantity* of loans available, rather than the interest-rate cost of obtaining them. There are various ways of controlling credit from the banks. The Government can insist on **special deposits**; the banks have to deposit millions of pounds of their cash at the Bank of England, so that they cannot lend it to customers. Or the Government can order the banks to put a ceiling on their lending. The problem is, though, that if people cannot borrow money from the banks they will simply get it from somewhere else. This process is called **disintermediation**, perhaps the ultimate in economic jargon. People can simply give each other credit, which is common among traders anyway, or they can borrow from friends and relatives. The end result may be that we have the same level of borrowing as before, only outside the banking system. Since the lending is outside the banking system, the Government cannot even measure it, let alone control it. Credit control policies can therefore be counterproductive, as was found when they were tried in the early 1970s.

Monetary policy in practice

Governments used to think monetary policy was less important than fiscal policy until the 1970s. The emphasis was on achieving certain public expenditure and taxation goals, with monetary policy being used in support. In the late 1970s this position was reversed because of the rise of the **monetarists**. The monetarists believed that increases in the money supply caused the inflation of the time; the secret therefore was to control the money supply. Both Labour after 1976 and the Conservatives since 1979 have tried to do this. The Thatcher Government set targets for the various monetary aggregates, mainly M1 and M3. Target ranges of 5–10% p.a. were usual early on, and later 2–6% p.a. However, it proved impossible to keep the aggregates down within the target ranges most of the time. Also, it was far from clear how the monetary aggregates were actually influencing inflation. The problem was that rapid developments in the financial system were changing the nature of the relationship between deposits (included in M1 and M3) and spending (and hence inflation). By 1987, the only monetary aggregate with an official target was M0, the cash base, whose target range was typically set at 1–5%. The relationship between cash and spending is obviously far more stable than that between deposits and spending.

Since the Government is trying to control purchasing power and spending to curb inflation, the best definition of money is the one which most strongly influences spending. This suggests that broader measures of money are more important than narrower ones. The trouble is that broad definitions are much less predictable than narrow ones. Changes in the financial system mean that broader money behaves in a different way and so the connection between broad money and spending or inflation is unreliable. The Government has reacted to this dilemma by maintaining narrow money targets (for M0) and abandoning broad money targets. However, it tries to bolster its anti-inflation policy by using high interest rates to squeeze credit money (and hence spending and inflation), even though it does not have formal targets for broad money measures which include the credit-making capabilities of the banks (such as M3).

Discussion points
1. Which is the best definition of money?
2. Is credit more important than cash?
3. Should the financial system be regulated more tightly?
4. Should the Bank of England be independent from the Government?

TRADE AND EXCHANGE RATE POLICIES

The Government's policies on trade and the exchange rate are mainly designed to keep our balance of payments with other countries under control. There are also connections, however, between the domestic monetary or fiscal policies and the foreign trade policy of the Government. Let's see what a Government needs to do about its balance of payments and then go on to explore ways of doing it. We can then consider how Government domestic and foreign policies are linked.

Balance of payments: deficits and surpluses

The balance of payments accounts total up our transactions with foreign countries. If we import (buy) more than we export (sell), we will have a deficit on our accounts. If we export more than we import there will be a surplus on our accounts. Both these situations are a problem. If we have a **balance of payments deficit** then we owe money to foreigners. We cannot just print pounds sterling (£) and use them to pay for our imports. It may come as a surprise to learn that foreigners don't necessarily want £. Foreigners cannot spend £, (except to buy British exports, or for tourism); and if foreigners wanted to buy lots of British exports we wouldn't have a deficit in the first place! So the only way to pay for a deficit is with gold or foreign currencies, such as dollars, yen, krone, or other currencies with even stranger names (zlotties in Poland). The Bank of England has reserves of gold and foreign currencies but these are limited. It can also borrow gold and foreign currencies from other Governments and the IMF but, again, this cannot go on forever. Sooner or later, the lenders will want to be paid back in their own currency. It is therefore clear that a balance of payments deficit cannot go on for ever. Sooner or later it must be eliminated.

There are also problems with a **balance of payments surplus**. To begin with, if a country is selling more than it buys it is consuming less than it could be consuming. The extra exports could be used by people at home, to enjoy a higher standard of living. A further problem is that if one country (Japan, West Germany) is in surplus, other countries (UK, USA) must be in deficit. If the deficit countries manage to eliminate their deficits, they will eliminate the surplus countries' surpluses too. This means that a surplus cannot be sustained in the long run either. However there is not the same pressure on a country with a balance of payments surplus to act. If it chooses, it can sit back and go on with its present policies until the deficit countries with which it trades take action to cure their deficits. The surplus country need do nothing itself.

Curing a balance of payments deficit

The most obvious way to cure a balance of payments deficit, as discussed earlier, is to restrict imports. Imports can be controlled by

- imposing **tariffs** (taxes on imports to raise their price)
- **quotas** (limit the number of imported goods allowed)
- **bureaucratic** delays.

These measures may give domestic industry an advantage by making it harder for imports to get into the country to compete with them. There is a natural temptation to resort to such action. In the long run, however, other countries are bound to retaliate and impose their own trade controls. Before long, all countries would be imposing controls (**protectionism**) and the volume of world trade will fall, as it did in the 1930s. We saw earlier how trade was likely to benefit from specialisation and competition; we are better off if we can prevent such trade wars from starting. The need for such a strategy prompted the creation of the General Agreement on Tariffs and Trade. The European Community is another organisation which aims to promote more free trade. The EC, however, does have significant trade barriers against non-member countries, especially the Japanese, so that free trade is only encouraged within Europe. The question is, how to find a policy that cures trade imbalances without reducing the volume of world trade?

One possible weapon is the exchange rate. This directly affects the price of exports and imports and so can be used to influence the total value of exports and imports. Suppose that the Government causes the exchange rate of £ to fall. (This is called **devaluation**.) Each £ is now worth fewer dollars, yen, francs etc. It therefore takes fewer dollars, yen or francs to buy £1 worth of British exports. In other words, our exports look cheaper to foreigners. At the same time, if each £ is worth fewer dollars, yen or francs, it takes more £ to buy an imported good from foreign countries. Imports therefore look more expensive to home consumers. After a devaluation, exports (being cheaper) will tend to increase, and imports (being more expensive) will tend to decrease.

In fact, the exchange rate will tend to move downwards automatically if there is a balance of payments deficit.

1. The deficit means that debit items (imports and capital outflows) exceed credit items (exports and capital inflows).

2. The debit items involve *supplying sterling* onto the foreign exchange markets, to buy foreign currency with which to pay for the imports or investment abroad.

3. The credit items involve a *demand for sterling* on the exchange markets, by foreigners who need sterling to pay for our exports.

4. A deficit therefore means that the supply of sterling exceeds the demand for sterling. With an excess supply of sterling on the market, foreign currency dealers will cut its price to sell off

their excess supply. The price of sterling, the exchange rate, therefore falls.

As it falls, equilibrium will tend to be restored. A lower exchange rate increases exports (credits) and reduces imports (debits).

The Government can also bring about a devaluation of the currency artificially by simply dumping lots of it on the foreign exchange markets. This will create an excess supply of £ and force dealers to cut their price of sterling to sell off the excess.

The reverse of all this is true for a country with a balance of payments surplus (Japan, West Germany). If it can increase the value of its currency this will cure a balance of payments surplus. An upward movement in the exchange rate of a currency is called **revaluation**. It makes exports more expensive and imports cheaper, the reverse of a devaluation. The result is fewer exports and more imports, until a balance of payments equilibrium is restored. Of course, as with the deficit country, the exchange rate moves automatically: a balance of payments surplus implies more credit items than debit items on the accounts. This means an excess of demand for the currency of that country over its supply. The result is an increase in price (revaluation).

The other point to remember is that any action by deficit countries affects the surplus countries. The devaluation of a deficit country's currency means that the surplus country's currency has experienced a revaluation at the same time: if a £ is worth fewer dollars, then a dollar must be worth more £ than before:

Before revaluation £1.00 = $2.00; or $1.00 = £0.50
After revaluation   £1.00 = $4.00; or $1.00 = £0.25

Need for exchange rate stability

Countries try to avoid excessive movements of their currency, however. If a currency starts to fall fast, there will be a panic on the exchange markets and everyone will rush to sell. This can cause not just a fall, but a collapse, until the currency becomes worthless. Once your currency becomes internationally worthless you can't buy any imports at all, unless you first sell exports to get hold of foreign currency. This is a very difficult position to be in; nearly all countries need imports of food, raw materials or manufactured goods which they cannot produce themselves. Currency collapse will also mean inflation at home. A fall in sterling forces us to pay more £ to buy each item of imports. In other words the price of imports in the shops rises. We also import a lot of raw materials, and the increased cost of these is likely to be passed on by manufacturers to consumers in higher prices.

One result of a strong *increase* in the value of a currency is that speculators rush to buy it. (Speculators really do have a remarkable resemblance to sheep, which presumably explains why they often drive the same make of German car and live in converted warehouses.) A rush to buy creates a massive inflow of capital. In most advanced countries, there are sophisticated international banking facilities. This means that foreign money quickly flows into the domestic financial system. Once there, it boosts the domestic money supply (in the case of the UK, it would appear in M3c). A big increase in the money supply can cause increased spending and hence inflation. It seems that we get inflation either way.

But apart from these worries, rapid movements in exchange rates create a risk of loss for traders, as we have already seen. Suppose the £ exchange rate against the German DM rises. This means each £ is worth more DM (and each DM is worth fewer £). Exporters might suddenly find that if they are selling something in Germany for DM10, this is now worth fewer £ than they had expected when planning the project. They could therefore end up making a loss. Currency risks discourage exporters. We are then more likely to get a balance of payments deficit and the world as a whole may end up with less trade, and a lower standard of living.

How international and domestic economies are linked

The Government's international policies are connected with its domestic policies in two ways. Firstly, its domestic policies can affect total consumer spending and therefore imports. Secondly, its monetary policies can affect interest rates and hence capital inflows. Consumer spending can be influenced by the Government in three ways. It can cut its own spending, reducing demand for goods and services including imports. It can increase taxes, leaving less in consumers' pockets to buy imports with. Finally, it can push up interest rates, making it harder to borrow money, so that there is less for consumers to spend on imports. The Government can use high interest rates to make depositing money in British banks more attractive to foreigners. This also makes British people less inclined to deposit money abroad. The effect of all these policies is to help balance up a payments deficit and support the value of the currency. Fewer imports means fewer debits on the accounts, and more capital inflows means more credits. This helps to create a healthy balance of payments. Since debits involve supplying £ on the foreign exchange markets and credits involve a demand for £, there is less supply and more demand for £. Result: a stronger price or exchange rate for £.

There can also be effects in the other direction: from the trade and exchange rate policies to the domestic economy. If the Government achieves more exports and fewer imports, there will be more demand for the output of domestic firms. Some firms will be selling more to foreigners, and others more to domestic consumers who switch from buying imports to home goods. The effects on output and employment are beneficial, though too much demand can lead to inflation.

UK trade policies in action
The UK has long supported free trade, through GATT and through its membership of the European Community. It has done so despite a relatively weak balance of payments since 1945. The weakness of its balance of payments has often led the Government to curb domestic demand to try to reduce imports (for instance in the 1960s, late 1970s and late 1980s). At the same time sterling has often been allowed to fall to make our exports look cheaper to foreigners (for instance in 1967, 1973, 1976). In response to the big balance of payments deficits of the late 1980s, however, the Government has tried to restrain the demand for imports *without* letting the exchange rate drop. This is because a dramatic fall in the exchange rate can be inflationary. High interest rates have been used both to restrain consumer spending on imports and to make sterling attractive. This creates a demand for sterling, thus maintaining a high price for sterling in the markets. It also attracts capital to help pay for our current account deficit. There is less of a crisis in dealing with the large balance of payments deficit in the late 1980s because of reserves of foreign currency accumulated during the early 1980s, when proceeds from North Sea oil created big balance of payments surpluses for a while.

Discussion points
1. Is a co-ordinated European economic policy better than a national policy?
2. Can we solve our balance of payments problems without damaging the domestic economy?
3. Is a balance of payments surplus really a good thing?

GOVERNMENT ECONOMIC POLICY IN PRACTICE

The basic economic objectives of any Government are similar:

- Governments want to ensure full employment so that everyone has a job.

- They also want to create as much growth as possible in the output of goods and services, so that the real living standards of the population increase.

- Governments like to keep inflation down because a spiral of rising prices and wages is unpopular.

- Finally, Governments have to prevent or cure a deficit on the balance of payments, so that the country is not in debt to the rest of the world.

The main areas of disagreement are about how to distribute the nation's wealth and income. We have already discussed the various policies that a Government can pursue: industrial, fiscal, monetary and trade. There have really been three different eras this century as far as economic policy is concerned. The first covers the period up to and including the second world war (1939–45), the second is the post war period up to the 1970s, and the third begins after that.

Pre-war economic policy
In the early 1900s economics was still a young subject; economists had even less of an idea what they were talking about than they do today. There had been relatively little analysis of the economy as a whole at the macro level. Such economic theory as there was focussed on the behaviour of individual consumers or firms. We saw early on how the behaviour of individual buyers and sellers tends to create equilibrium in any market. Surely this theory would work just as well for the economy as a whole? The prevalent thinking in Government economic policy was therefore to leave the economy alone, and interfere with it as little as possible.

The results were catastrophic. In 1929 a financial collapse which began on Wall Street made hundreds of banks bankrupt. With banks gone, bank balances were wiped out and the result was a massive reduction in the world's money supply. This left people with much less purchasing power so, of course, total spending was drastically reduced. Faced with so much less demand, firms cut back on production or closed down for good, creating widespread unemployment. Rising unemployment meant there was even less income to buy things with, so the recession got worse. Since most economists at the time believed that the economy would restore itself to equilibrium if left to its own devices, the initial reaction of Governments was to do nothing. The recession began to get even worse.

Eventually Governments *had* to react. They did so by cutting industrial wages, putting up trade barriers, and devaluing the exchange rate. The object of wage cuts was to restore equilibrium in the labour market. Unemployment represents surplus labour (supply of labour exceeds demand for labour at the current wage). In any market, the way to sell off a surplus is to cut the price, in this case the wage. But this theory contained a major fallacy. In theory a cut in wages means that firms can afford to employ more workers. In practice a cut in wages means that consumers have less income, their demand for products is reduced, and firms have to cut back even more on production. This discourages them from employing workers even if workers are cheaper to hire, and some firms are likely to go under because of the loss of business. The failure to stimulate recovery made matters even worse.

The Government wanted to protect domestic industries and home employment; they put up tariffs and devalued exchange rates to make imports more expensive. If people were discouraged from buying imports, in theory they would buy more from British firms. In practice, of course, if every country plays this game, *everyone's* exports suffer. This means that even if more home consumers buy British products, fewer foreign consumers do, so in the end things don't improve and may even get worse (some industries were mainly exporters with limited demand from home consumers). Again, such policies failed to stimulate recovery. Even economists can learn from experience, however, eventually, and by this time many were beginning to question traditional theory. Some Governments now began to experiment with less orthodox policies.

Post war economic policies

By the early 1930s the British economist John Maynard Keynes was writing his famous book *General Theory of Employment, Interest and Money*. Some Governments had already begun to boost demand in their economies through Government spending, the best known example being President Roosevelt's 'New Deal' in the USA. The idea was very simple. High unemployment could not be cured by expecting the price in the labour market (the wage rate) to adjust to equilibrium in the normal way, nor by forcing it down artificially. A lower wage meant even less demand by consumers and so even less production and employment. Even if labour is cheaper, firms will not employ more of it in these circumstances.

The only answer was to increase the demand for goods and services directly through Government action; firms would then want to produce more and so would need to employ more labour. Keynes therefore advocated **deficit spending**: increasing Government spending without increasing taxes. The Government's financial deficit is then covered by borrowing, or by printing money (mainly by borrowing). Roosevelt's programme of 'public works' (eg the building of roads financed by the Government) was an example of 'Keynesian' policy before Keynes, since the New Deal began in 1932 and Keynes' *General Theory* was not published until 1936. Following this, entirely by accident, there was a massive increase in Government spending during the 1939–45 War, which of course amounted to Keynesian deficit spending on a grand scale. The enlistment of men going to fight helped employment still further and so the era of mass unemployment finally passed.

Post war UK economic policy was set out in the 1944 White Paper *Employment Policy*, produced by the wartime coalition Government. This policy came to be known as **demand management**. It involved influencing the level of demand in the economy through Government spending and taxation. The primary aim was to ensure high employment: if people demand lots of products, lots of workers will be needed to produce them. The White Paper foresaw that there might be problems with demand management. We know from looking at inflation earlier that too much demand is a major cause of inflation. In practice it proved easier than expected to maintain high demand and full employment, without creating inflation. Throughout the 1950s and 1960s employment levels remained higher than the authors of the White Paper had hoped for, and inflation averaged only 3% in the 1950s and 4% in the 1960s. There were occasional balance of payments difficulties (since the high demand sucked in too many imports) and a few complaints from industry about Government intervention. There were no serious difficulties, however, until the 1970s.

Part of the 1944 White Paper plan was to create a large staff of economists and statisticians at the Treasury to provide accurate statistics and forecasts on which to base the demand management policies. Previously, Government policy had been not to interfere, and so there had been no need for statistical information. To carry out demand management policies it was necessary not only to have accurate information about what had happened, but also to forecast what was going to happen. This is because it can take several months for a Government's economic policies to take effect, and it needs to know what things will be like in the future. Since economists can't even agree what the situation is now, this is asking a lot. Nevertheless, millions of pounds of taxpayers' money is spent trying.

The years of demand management were not without problems, however. The increases in demand, to maintain full employment, often led to excessive imports, as people spent some of the extra money in the economy on foreign goods which they believed were of better quality. To curb these imports the Government had to devalue the pound to make imports more expensive and exports cheaper. It also had to restrain demand occasionally to curtail imports. This obviously reversed the whole point of demand management policies, and created what became known as **stop-go** cycles. Industrialists complained that constant intervention by the Government created instability and made it hard for them to plan ahead. The need for constant action arose partly because of the balance of payments problem and partly because, despite the statistical forecasts, the Government never had an accurate enough picture of what was going to happen to know what to do about it. The most serious problem was the inflationary pressure which took off in the 1970s. By creating a full employment guarantee the Government was giving the trades unions a blank cheque. The unions could claim more or less whatever wage increases they liked. If firms laid off workers because employing them was too expensive, then the Government would create enough demand to re-employ them all again (at even higher wages).

In 1973 when oil prices rose sharply, industry's costs rose dramatically so they put up the prices in the shops. Unions reacted by claiming huge pay rises to try to keep ahead of the game. They realised this would make it harder for firms to employ people, but they expected that the Government would go on creating enough demand to ensure full employment. In fact the Government action to increase demand simply meant even more inflation. By the mid 1970s, inflation was over 20% and getting out of control. It is very hard to curb inflation without reducing demand, and Governments were committed to sustaining demand in order to maintain full employment. The problem was not so much the idea of managing demand, but simply that demand was being managed at the wrong level. A lower level of demand was needed to cure inflation, but unfortunately the Government was committed to full employment, which meant a higher level of demand.

1979: the beginning of Thatcherism

The Conservative Government in 1979 found itself faced with a similar inflationary crisis. The previous Labour Government had tried to hold down inflation by cutting demand (by reducing Government spending) and by voluntary wage restraint. These policies had just broken down, and there had been another rise in oil prices and another round of big wage increases. The only way out seemed to be to abandon the full employment commitment altogether. The Government announced that its first priority would be to reduce inflation. It imposed tight control of demand through control of the money supply. It kept tight control of Government spending and put up interest rates to make it harder for people to get money for their own spending. The Government argued that if inflation continued it would destroy jobs anyway; economic instability would discourage businesses from investing in new production facilities or even replacing worn out ones.

The result of this tight control of demand was, not surprisingly, high unemployment. High unemployment meant less income and so less demand, which in turn lessened the inflationary pressure. Rising unemployment also frightened the unions into making smaller wage claims. High wages could well drive your firm out of business and, with 3 million out of work, finding another job might be very difficult. By 1985 inflation had fallen to just 3%. The high interest rates in the early Thatcher years helped to make sterling an attractive investment. This created a demand for sterling which meant that its price (the exchange rate) remained high. A high exchange rate makes import prices cheaper, which helps to keep inflation down. However, it also makes exports more expensive and therefore harder to sell, which keeps unemployment high.

Of course, we cannot just stand by and allow an unemployment rate of 3 million to continue. Aside from individual hardship, it means massive wasted resources. If we cannot cure the problem by creating more demand, we need some other policy. The Thatcher philosophy was to encourage more enterprise in the economy. Enterprise creates growth in the economy from the supply side. Unlike extra demand, which encourages prices to rise, extra supply in the economy encourages them to fall. To sell the extra supply of products, firms need to lower their prices. The result is more sales, output and therefore employment. This seems to have worked well between 1986–88, when output rose sharply and unemployment fell rapidly (to 1.6m by 1989).

In 1988, however, the economy showed signs of 'overheating'. In other words demand was rising too fast and firms could not expand their supply of goods and services fast enough to keep up. As a result, imports were sucked in from abroad (creating a balance of payments problem) and domestic firms increased their prices because they had plenty of customers (creating inflation). Consumer spending rose sharply in 1988 because of tax cuts and because of low interest rates (designed to help financial institutions ride out the effects of the stock market crash of 1987). The renewed burst of inflation (reaching 8%) and the growing balance of payments deficit forced the Government to re-impose its tight money, high interest rate policies of the early 1980s.

7

Economics and Your Money

YOU AND YOUR MONEY

We all rather take money for granted. But it's like everything else, if you take it for granted you may end up losing it. Careful management of your money can ensure that you get the most out of it and don't run into financial problems. This section will be divided into three main areas. The first is spending money, which you may think you're quite good at already! The second is saving and investing money. The final area covers various legal matters.

Spending money

The need to be careful with money is something that people appreciated rather more in the past than we do now. Our higher standard of living has made money less crucial, but it is still a very important matter to most people. Most of us have a limited income which cannot buy all the things we might like (Porsche, trip to Florida, case of vintage burgundy, etc). The key to successful spending is to budget carefully, so that you buy the things which are actually most useful to you. To take an extreme example, it would be silly to spend £10,000 on a second hand Porsche, only to find that you have too little left over to pay the electricity bill next winter. The best idea is to make a list of all the things you need to buy. Obviously, things like food, clothing, accommodation (rent or mortgage), household bills (electricity, etc) and travel costs, must come at the top. Then add to the list in order of importance various luxuries, such as nights out, holiday, car. Work out the total cost of each thing on the list and your total income and see how far down the list you can comfortably get. This process will ensure that you spend your money on what is most important to you.

You can do this for a year ahead, but to ensure that what you *plan* to spend on each thing is what you *actually* spend, you need to convert your list into a weekly budget. Unless you specify a weekly amount to spend on things like nights out or groceries, you will soon find that you go over budget. There should also be some savings in your budget, at least 10% of the total. This is because you'll probably end up going over the budget sooner or later anyway. As soon as you meet scintillating Susie or dashing Derek, your budget for nightlife will go straight out the window. Or perhaps the car unexpectedly breaks down and needs repairs. Savings can be used to bridge the gap when unexpected spending is needed. If substantial savings accumulate they can then be used to buy something special, such as a video recorder or a weekend in Paris. Without a savings element in your budget you will fritter that money away on things like beer and have nothing left to show for it.

Being careful with money does not have to mean being frugal. Most of us will earn a considerable sum during our lifetimes, but usually this is spread over many years, with earnings tending to be higher in later life. Spending, on the other hand, is usually more pressing when you are younger, to have a good time or to raise a family. There is therefore a mismatch between the time when most money is earned and the time when most of it is spent. The obvious answer is to borrow. Most people borrow money to buy their home, and for other expensive items such as cars. Borrowing to buy a home involves taking out a mortgage, a loan using the house or flat as security. Building societies specialise in this, but there are mortgage brokers in most towns who can advise you where to get the best deal. Most building societies will only lend three times your annual income. Although other organisations will lend more, the building society rule is sensible. If you borrow more than three times your income you may find it very hard to keep up the monthly repayments, especially if the interest rate goes up.

For smaller items, borrowing may take many forms. The most common are:

- bank overdraft
- bank loan
- finance deal
- credit card.

A **bank overdraft** involves arranging with your bank to spend more money than you have in your account. Interest is added monthly or quarterly to the outstanding debt. The interest rate is quite high, but this way of borrowing has the advantage of flexibility. You can overdraw any amount up to the agreed limit but only pay interest on the amount you actually use.

With a fixed **loan**, you pay interest on the whole amount for the whole period of the agreement. Now, of course, if you borrow £1,000 to be repaid over two years you don't really borrow £1,000 for two years: you start paying it back at the end of the very first month, so that most of it is borrowed for much less than two years. Adding interest to the whole £1,000 for the whole two years means you pay about double the interest you should pay. Suppose 10% interest is used in the calculation or £100 a year; you are really paying about 20%, because after the first year the outstanding debt may only be about £500.

The true interest payment is called the **Annual Percentage Rate** (APR) and this must be displayed by law on any finance agreement. This is the rate which you need to compare with the interest rate on bank overdrafts. Remember that if you decide to settle a fixed loan early, you may still have to pay some of the interest beyond the settlement date, unlike an overdraft. On the other hand, there is often an 'arrangement fee' for an overdraft, typically ½% to 2% of the amount. Car dealers and suppliers of large items like fitted kitchens, have their own finance arrangements with finance companies. These loans are just like fixed bank loans, and sometimes they may be available at very cheap interest rates (especially for cars).

Credit cards are rather like permanent overdraft facilities which you can spend by signing a slip of paper. The wise thing to do with credit cards, however, is to use them as a substitute for cash but settle the outstanding account each month. If you get into debt on your credit card, you will find that the interest amounts to something quite horrifying, sometimes more than 30% APR.

It is useful to remember the laws of supply and demand when spending money, whether it is borrowed or not. If you want to buy a house, it is usually better to buy as soon as you can since prices tend to keep rising. Prices rise in the long term as more people are trying to buy and people have higher incomes, all of which creates a strong demand in the housing market. On the other hand, some of the best bargains can be had during the rare periods when the housing market is weak and few people can afford to buy (in 1989–1990 for instance when high interest payments made house buying difficult). When buying cars, it is worth trying to find a make of car which is in demand second hand. It will keep its value much better, and the cost savings can be immense. German cars are particularly good in this respect. You can also bargain over the price of large

items like houses and cars. If sellers are anxious to trade you can
negotiate large discounts. This is true in house buying (except
when the market is very strong and everyone wants to buy) and it
is often true for cars. When car dealers are facing sluggish demand
and lots of competition, they will often give big cash discounts
(though to get these you will have to dispose of your existing car
privately to avoid a trade in), and may also provide very cheap
finance. It is always worth taking your time and shopping around.

Your savings and investments

Savings and investments are perhaps the most confusing areas of
finance for most people. Of course, some people barely have
enough money to spend and don't need to worry about saving or
investing it. The obvious forms of saving are bank deposits and
building society or post office accounts. There are also things like
unit trusts and life assurance policies linked to unit trusts. Buying a
house, or other property, is also a form of saving and investment,
even if you have to borrow the money to pay for it. When you are
saving smaller sums of money (less than £5,000) or for short
periods (less than three years), the best thing is to use a building
society or bank. Shop around for the best rate of interest and the
scheme which suits you. Banks and building societies offer high
interest accounts or bonds if you want to deposit large amounts for
long periods.

However, for large sums (more than £5,000) or long term
purposes (longer than three years), unit trusts are usually better.
A unit trust scheme takes money from thousands of people to
build a fund running into millions. Investing on this scale, the fund
managers can spread the money across a range of shares, bonds or
property. This spread lessens the risk of losses. Even if there is a
stock market collapse, much of the money is in property and
Government bonds, whose value tends to rise during a stock
market collapse. It is also a fair bet that the fund managers have
far more expertise in making investments than most other people,
including economists. Since it is their job, they obviously have
more experience and time to research potential investments carefully. Sometimes unit trusts can rise in value quite dramatically,
though they do occasionally fall as well. It depends on the general
state of the world economy. In prosperous times, companies do
well and the value of shares rises. Even in a recession, however, a
unit trust fund spread across various bonds and property, as well as
shares, tends to hold up well. Ask what the fund is actually

invested in and try to decide how much risk you want to take (shares are riskier but potentially more profitable than bonds).

A particularly useful variation is a life assurance policy linked to unit trusts, sometimes called an **endowment policy**. This gives you life assurance cover and (assuming you survive) a lump sum, tax free, after say ten years. To find out about unit trusts with or without life assurance, ask local insurance companies or banks. See which funds have performed well in the past. The *Investors Chronicle* is a good source of independent advice.

Another area of increasing importance is **pensions**. In addition to the state pension and various occupational pensions provided by employers, there are also private pension schemes, often organised by insurance companies. It may be worth looking into these, though good occupational schemes, such as the one for teachers, are often best. Pension funds like insurance funds are invested in unit trusts; the fund managers try to ensure there is lots of money available to pay you a good pension at the end.

They always make sure that enough of the money is invested safely so that even in an economic recession there should be no problem.

Your money and the law

Taxation is something which most people do not need to worry about, since it is deducted automatically by employers through **Pay As You Earn** (PAYE). National insurance contributions are deducted in the same way. You should check that they are deducting the right amount, though. Each year the Inland Revenue will send you a notification telling you what your tax code is. If you have any doubts, contact them and they will tell you whether you are entitled to a more generous code. Everyone is entitled to basic personal allowances. Parents get allowances for children. You may also be entitled to extra allowances for dependent relatives or disabilities. If you are self employed, or have income from investments (eg rented housing), you should see an accountant for expert advice on how to minimise your tax bill. The accountant has a wide range of techniques to help you, and it's surprising just how little you've earned when he finishes. Remember, though, it's your responsibility to declare your income to the Inland Revenue, and failure to do so is a criminal offence.

The only other aspect of your personal finance which may bring you in contact with the law is poor merchandise. Goods bought must be fit for the purpose for which they are sold; if they are not, you are entitled to a full cash refund. If the shop won't play ball,

write a letter pointing out that, under the Sale of Goods Act, you
should be given your money back. If this does not do the trick, you
may consider taking the shop to the Small Claims Court. This is
quite easy. Just go to the nearest County Court and say you want
to take out a summons in the Small Claims Court. The forms are
fairly straightforward and the cost is very small. If you have any
difficulties consult a Citizens Advice Bureau. Remember, if you
have a low income and few savings you will be entitled to free legal
aid from a solicitor. Ask about this at your Citizens Advice
Bureau, too.

RUNNING A BUSINESS

The number of people starting their own business in the UK grew
dramatically during the 1980s, encouraged by the Thatcher Government's 'enterprise culture'. Starting a business is a kind of
gamble. Potentially, a great deal of money could be made. At the
same time, however, there is a risk of substantial loss. How you
play percentages is a personal matter, of course. You may like
taking chances; you may not. Your circumstances will also be
important, though again this depends on you. Having a young
family may discourage you from starting a business, or it may spur
you on. Assuming you do decide to set up, there are a few key
problems you have to solve.

Finding a product or service to sell

Firstly, you have to find a viable proposition. Have you got an idea
for a product or service that you can sell? It doesn't have to be a
new idea, or even a new form of an old idea. It can be just another
example of something that already exists done better or done in a
new place. It's pretty obvious what *not* to do (selling caviar to
down-and-outs under Charing Cross Bridge), but it's less clear
what *will* attract customers. Even if there are customers for your
idea, are there enough of them? And what about existing competitors in that market; how many are there and how strong are they?

If you still think you have a viable project you need to decide
the form your business should take. Should you be a sole trader, or
have partners, or set up a limited company? You ought to take
legal advice on the setting up of partnerships or companies. You
will need to research your market to find out exactly what the
customers want and then promote your product or service to those
customers. Running the business will involve dealing on a daily
basis with all sorts of paperwork, including tax returns, salaries

and financial control. You will also have to manage the people you work with—no easy matter in itself.

Your business and the economy

Each aspect of running a business needs detailed and expert explanation and this book is not the place for that. If you are serious about starting a business, read some of the many books which have been written recently about the subject. Ask for advice from anyone who might be able to help, including your bank manager, accountant, solicitor or anyone you know in business.

The one thing economists can advise you on is the connection between your business and the economy. Clearly, if the economy is booming and output is rising, there will be plenty of employment and incomes will be high. This will mean strong demand for most products and services. Businesses need to prepare for this by increasing productive capacity. Alternatively, you may be able to charge higher prices if customers have more money to spend, but this depends on your competition. If there are lots of firms competing for customers, raising prices will be difficult even in a boom.

The reverse of all this is also true: if we expect a recession you should be ready to reduce output and if necessary employment too. Read the serious press to get some idea of how economic developments might affect your business. If you sell a lot of your products to tourists, for example, and the exchange rate for sterling is rising, you could be in for problems. A highly valued £ means foreigners have to pay a lot for British goods, so you may lose custom. If interest rates are high, people are less likely to buy the sorts of things they normally borrow money for, like cars or fitted kitchens. If taxes have just been cut and the general standard of living is rising, then people will be more inclined to spend money on luxuries, like restaurants. You can keep one step ahead of these developments if you understand the basic workings of the economy.

8
A Bit of Maths

PERCENTAGES, GRAPHS AND AVERAGES

Some of you may be perfectly happy with maths, even at a high level, in which case you can skip this chapter altogether. Most readers, however, will probably not be in this category. The problem with maths is that most people have a kind of phobia about it. On a scale of fright, it probably ranks somewhere between werewolves and a visit to the dentist. Psychologists have carried out experiments to see how people do at basic maths when they think it *isn't* maths. Two groups were given essentially the same problems to solve, one in pure mathematical form, the other expressed in practical terms (apples and oranges, say). The latter group always performed much better than the former. To a large extent, therefore, it's simply a fear of maths that makes people incapable of doing it. A little more confidence is in order! To get a basic grasp of economics, you need a bit of simple maths. For those of you who think 'simple maths' is a contradiction in terms, this chapter will put the ideas across in the plainest possible English.

Percentages

Percentages, first of all: a percentage is simply a fraction or a part of something. 'Per cent' simply means 'per hundred'. Let's say that Bros get a 10 per cent (10%) royalty from their 'Greatest Hits' album, and that the album sells at £5, or 500p. We divide this into a hundred equal bits. Each bit will be 5p (to divide by a hundred just knock off two noughts). The singer gets 10 of these bits, in other words 50p.

Suppose there are 25 million people of working age in the UK (25,000,000) and 8% of them are unemployed. What number are unemployed? We divide the 25 million into a hundred equal bits, which makes each bit 250,000. Now 8% of 25 million means 8 of

170

these 250,000 bits. 8 times 250,000 is 2,000,000 or 2 million, the number of unemployed.

Suppose a car costs £8,000, and then prices rise by 5%. What is the new price? We must first work out what 5% of £8,000 is, and then add it on. If we divide £8,000 into a hundred equal bits we get £80. Now 5% means five of these bits; 5 times £80 comes to £400. So for a 5% price increase we add this £400 to the original £8,000, giving £8,400. (For a 5% cash discount, we would take away the £400 from the original £8,000 to get £7,600.)

These are fairly easy numbers, but the principle is just the same with more difficult figures. To find a percentage of any number, first divide it by 100. This tells you what *one* per cent of that number is. Then simply multiply this by the percentage you want. If, by now, you're wondering what the point of all this is, it's just a way of expressing a fraction or part of something. Obviously, 50% is a half, 25% is a quarter, 70% is 'most' of whatever we're talking about, 90% is 'nearly all' of it. The idea is to express the fraction or part of a number that we are talking about in a form which is easy to understand, and easy to compare.

Graphs

Graphs next. A graph is simply a picture which shows the connection between two things. The idea is to depict how two connected things *change* in response to one another. If one changes, the other will change. To make a graph, we simply draw two lines, one vertical and the other horizontal. We measure one of our two things along the vertical, and the other along the horizontal. We then mark points showing the levels of the two things that go together. Joining up these points produces our graph.

Let's take an example. Suppose we want to show the connection between the air temperature and the number of people sunbathing on the beach at Bognor. Suppose one day the temperature is 75 degrees and we count 8,000 people on the beach at noon. On the graph we plot (draw) point A, at a level of 75 degrees on the temperature line and 8,000 on the sunbathers line. Another day, say, the temperature is 70 degrees and only 7,000 people are on the beach at noon. We plot point B on the graph to mark this changed level of temperature and sunbathers. We go on plotting more points in the same way. Joining up all the different points we noted gives us a graph. What does the graph show? In this case it shows that, as the temperature rises, more people go down to the beach to sunbathe.

Some more examples might help. We might draw a graph

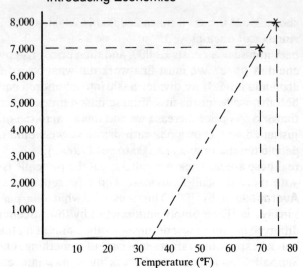

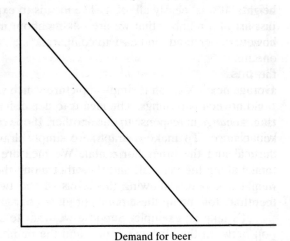

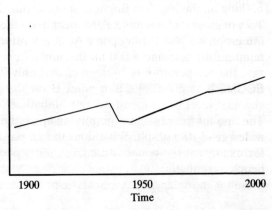

showing what happens to the demand for pints of beer as the price rises. Obviously, at higher prices, people will be less able to afford beer and may buy some other drink instead. In the same way, we could draw a graph showing what happens to total incomes in the economy as time progresses. As time goes on, economies tend to become more productive, though there are occasional dips as things go wrong from time to time. Like percentages, graphs are just another way of presenting information to make it easier for people to understand. The graph makes things easier, because it is really a picture.

Averages
Finally, averages. An average attempts to summarise a list of different numbers with a single number. This may sound ridiculous but it is easy enough to see the point with a simple example. Suppose that I have fifteen students in my class, all of different heights. If someone asks me, 'How tall are your students?', I could just list all their heights. This would give too much information, however, and could be confusing. We want to answer by giving one number only, which in some way conveniently represents all the heights of all the students. This one number is called the average height.

So how do we calculate the average of a list of numbers? Let's take another example. Suppose five of us have each bought a kebab from Stavros and we want to know the average weight of these five kebabs. We could stick all five together and then cut the total into five equal bits, and weigh one of those pieces. That weight would be the average. The way to calculate an average is therefore to

- add up all the things whose average we want
- then divide by the number of things we have.

To work out the average height of fifteen students, we add up all fifteen heights and then divide the total by fifteen. We then get one number, the 'average' of all fifteen heights.

ECONOMIC STATISTICS

The use of percentages, graphs and averages in economics is widespread. Many statistics are given in a simple numerical form, for example the unemployment figures, showing the number of people out of work and claiming benefit. Other simple figures are those for the balance of payments current account, giving the total value of the deficit (or surplus) in £. Likewise, the national income accounts are expressed in £. Many statistics, however, require the use of **percentage** changes, for instance interest rates. For example we say interest rates go up from 10% to 12%. The interest rate is the fraction of a loan or deposit which is added on by the bank or building society. We also express changes in key economic statistics in percentages. The growth of the economy (increase in national output or income) is given in terms of an annual percentage change. We say GDP for example has increased by 2.3%. **Graphs** are widespread in economic statistics, being used most often to show changes over time in all sorts of things. **Averages** are commonly used for all sorts of economic statistics too, including average income per person, average house prices, average output per worker in manufacturing, and so on.

Index numbers in economics

Perhaps the most confusing economic statistics are those which involve a combination of percentages, graphs and averages. One important example is the Retail Price Index, which measures the rate of inflation; another is the infamous Financial Times-Stock Exchange 100 Share Index, which measures the level of share prices on the Stock Exchange (and which nobody seems to understand). There is also a 'Sterling Index', which measures the value of the exchange rate. The value of an index is always changing, so it is often shown on a graph as well. An index is usually calculated so that it begins at a base number such as 100 or sometimes 1000. Let's look at these examples more closely.

The Retail Price Index

The Retail Price Index (RPI) is used to measure inflation, in other words changes in the general level of retail prices in the economy. To represent all prices throughout the economy in a single figure we obviously need an average. Now, it would be impossible to measure the average price of every single thing on sale in the UK. We therefore conduct a Household Expenditure Survey to find out what most families spend most of their money on. We then use this information to construct a monthly 'basket' of several hundred commodities, including food, clothing, entertainments, petrol and mortgages. With important things like bread, there may be more than one in the basket. This imaginary basket is supposed to represent consumer spending in the UK and we can easily calculate the average price of everything in it. Suppose that the answer is £5 (in other words, the average price of all the various things in the basket is £5 per item). For the sake of convenience, we call the answer in the first year 100. Whatever the actual number is (in this example £5) we re-name it, so to speak, as 100. In the following years, we calculate the average cost of the things in the basket again. Suppose that it rises from £5 to £5.50. This is an increase of 10% and so our index rises from 100 to 110. The RPI would then be 110 and the rate of inflation 10%. This calculation involves finding an *average* figure for prices and calculating the *percentage* change in that figure. The changes can easily be *graphed* if so desired. Calling the answer 100 at the beginning just makes it easier to see what the percentage change is as time progresses. Of course, once the answer has risen considerably, to say 250 or more, it becomes hard to see at a glance what the percentage change is. To get round this problem, and to update the basket of commodities, we start again. Every few years we change the basket and call the current year's answer 100. If prices rise by 5% next year the RPI would then become 105 and so on.

The FTSE 100 Index

The Financial Times-Stock Exchange 100 Share Index (FTSE100) is the same kind of thing as the RPI. It measures the average price of 100 leading shares on the Stock Exchange. Just as the basket of commodities in the RPI represents all the commodities in the economy, so the 100 shares are supposed to represent all the shares on the Stock Exchange. When the FTSE ('Footsie') was first introduced in 1984, the average price of the 100 shares was calculated. The original answer was then called 1000. As the average prices rose during the years that followed the index rose too, reaching 2400 at one point in 1987, before falling back to 1700 after the Great Crash. The FTSE100 is often quoted on the news and in the papers. With this particular index the figure is not put back to 1000 every so often, but merely continues from its original base figure. If the average price of the 100 shares eventually becomes five times what it was in 1984, then the FTS100 would rise to 5000 and so on. It gives everyone a quick impression of how Stock Exchange prices are moving.

The Sterling Index

Similarly, the Sterling Index is a way of calculating the average value of the pound against the currencies of our main trading partners; it started off with 1985 = 100. If all this business of index numbers is confusing, the basic idea is simple. We calculate an average, call it an index set at 100 (or 1000) and then show changes using this index. The index is just a convenient way of representing a mass of statistics in one figure. If the FTSE100 rises from 2000 to 2050, this shows a significant increase in share prices on average. The basic idea, if not the method of calculation, is therefore quite simple.

9
Conclusion

WHERE TO GO FROM HERE

Hopefully, we have come to see that the basic ideas of economics are really quite straightforward. It is only because economists rather enjoy elaborate language that we find it so hard to understand them. The fact that economics cannot be conducted like a proper science means that what economists say may not be entirely accurate. This is not an excuse, however, for them to say things in a way which cannot be understood. Nor should any economist pretend to know exactly what is going on. Economic processes can never be exactly explained, since they are so bound up with human behaviour. Human behaviour changes from time to time and place to place, so economic processes can never be predictable. Any forecasts from any economist are therefore always liable to be inaccurate and economists should recognise this.

Does all this mean that economics is a waste of time? Not at all—economics does enable us to get a rough idea of what is going on and to make some predictions about the future. It is certainly true that economic theory and statistical methods can be improved. As the subject develops it may give us a clearer insight into, and more accurate forecasts about, the economy.

For many people who are just interested in the subject, or who need a basic understanding for a course on economics or related subjects (such as sociology), the contents of this book may be enough. If you want to further your understanding of economics there are a number of options. Evening classes at a local college leading to A-level Economics are one possibility; further reading is another. The list of books in the suggestions for further reading is by no means comprehensive. The list is divided into economic theory and applied economics. If you are just interested in what goes on in the world, look out for the applied economics books. If you are studying economics or some related course at school or college, you will need the theory. The appropriate level of theory depends on your course and you should seek further advice from your teachers. Good luck!

Further Reading

Free Goodies
Available absolutely free of charge (just apply direct to the organisations concerned, saying that you are a student of economics):
The Lloyds Bank Review
The Barclays Bank Review
The Midland Bank Review
The Nat West Bank Review
The Royal Bank of Scotland Review & Summary of UK Business Conditions
The Treasury's Economic Progress Report
The Bank of England Briefing

Economic Theory
Introduction to Economics, Cairncross
Economics, Livesey
Economics a New Approach, Anderton
Economics, Harrison
Introductory Economics, Stanlake
A Textbook of Economic Analysis, Nevin
Introduction to Modern Economics, Hardwick
Modern Economics, Heathfield
Economics, Begg
Positive Economics, Lipsey

Applied Economics
Introduction to the UK Economy, Harbury & Lipsey
Understanding the Economy, Dunnett
The British Economy, Peston
The UK Economy, Prest & Coppock
Applied Economics, Griffiths & Wall
Economics and the Economy, Jeffreys
An Introduction to British Economic Policy, Hare & Kirby

Investigating Economics, Hockey & Powell
The Times on the Economy, Williams
The UK Economy, the National Institute of Economic & Social
   Research

Glossary

APR   Annual Percentage Rate of interest on a loan.

Barter   Trade by swapping goods.

Balance of Payments   The accounts of one country's trade with the rest of the world.

Communism   A social system based on a planned economy and equal income distribution.

Complements   Goods consumed together.

Co-operative   A firm owned by its workers or by its consumers.

Customs   Taxes on imports. Also called tariffs.

Deflation   A fall in prices generally (including wages) throughout the economy. The opposite of **inflation**.

Demand   The amount of goods and services people try to buy at various price levels. The opposite of **supply**.

Economies of scale   Savings of costs per unit of production which are achieved as output increases.

ECU   European Currency Unit.

Equilibrium   Position of stability, or balance, with no tendency for change.

European Community (EC)   Collection of European countries co-operating to provide trade.

European Monetary System (EMS)   The system for fixing the **exchange rates** of European currencies.

Exchange rate   The value of one national currency expressed in terms of another.

Free market   Market in which people and firms can trade without restrictions or regulations.

FTSE100 Index   Average price of 100 leading shares on the UK **Stock Exchange**. The original index base in 1984 was 1000. The index is nicknamed 'Footsie'.

Growth   Increase in the output of real goods and services (eg allowing for **inflation**).

Inflation Increase in prices generally (including wages) through the economy. The opposite of **deflation**.

Infrastructure The physical framework on which the economy rests, such as roads, houses, schools, hospitals and sewerage.

Keynesians and **monetarists** Two different schools of thought on the subject of **macro-economics** and economic management.

Legal tender A form of payment which people are bound by law to accept.

Limited company A form of business organisation which has a legal and financial identity quite separate from its owners.

Liquidity The ease with which a form of money or asset can be spent.

Macro-economics The study of the economy as a whole. See also **micro-economics**.

Merchant banks Banks which make large longterm loans to companies. Also known as investment banks.

Micro-economics Study of the economic activity of individual people or firms. See also **macro-economics**.

Monetarists See **Keynesians**.

Monopolies and Mergers Commission (MMC) Official body which decides whether a merger between companies would be in the public interest.

Multinational A company which *produces* in more than one country.

Nationalised industry A large business enterprise owned by the Government.

Planned economy An economy in which the Government decides trade.

PLC A public limited company, one whose shares are quoted and traded on the **Stock Exchange**.

Price mechanism The means by which the price level is established.

Privatised industry A former **nationalised industry** sold off by the Government to private shareholders.

Stock Exchange A place where shares and bonds are bought and sold secondhand.

Substitutes Alternative goods.

Supply The amount of goods and services people try to sell at various price levels. The opposite of **demand**.

Trade Union A collection of workers who have united so as to negotiate with their employer jointly.

Utility The economist's term for the satisfaction people gain from consuming something.

Index

More Books for Business Studies

The following pages contain details of a selection of other titles of interest to students in Economics, Business Studies, Accountancy and Finance. For further information, and details of our Inspection Copy Service, please apply to:

Northcote House Publishers Ltd, Plymbridge House, Estover Road, Plymouth PL6 7PZ, United Kingdom. Tel: Plymouth (0752) 705251. Fax: (0752) 777603. Telex: 45635.

A selection of catalogues is usually available on request.

Core Business Studies Series
General Editor: Eddie Martin OStJ MSc DMS MBIM

The popular series of pocket guides for students starting or revising courses in Business Studies, Economics, and Accountancy and Finance. Presented in a smart pocket-sized format, the Series offers the professional approach: practical, structured, realistic, integrated, and complete with Q & A material and imaginative minicases.

Computer Programming
J R Firth MA

Computer Studies
D Hawgood MA MInstP
  MBCS

Economics
Roger Maile BA CertEd

Finance
D A Harvey BSc(Econ) MSc
  IPFA

Management Accounting
D A Harvey BSc(Econ) MSc
  IPFA & M Nettleton
  BSc(Econ)

Marketing
E T Martin OStJ MSc DMS
  MBIM

Operational Research
P Harrison MSc DMS MBIM

Organization Theory
P Bryans BA MSc(Econ) & T
  P Cronin BA MSc(Econ)

Production
R Hunter MSc CertEd DMS
  MIMS

Statistics
E T Martin OSt MSc DMS
  MBIM & J R Firth MA

Each pocket-sized hardback, 128 pages, illustrated.

Starting Business Studies
John Frain

A concise introduction for young people to the increasingly popular but complex world of business, management and professional studies in further and higher education. Dr Frain is Principal of South Mersey College Liverpool, and has held many distinguished appointments in the field of business education.

Paperback, 144 pages, illustrated.

The Big Bang
Guy Galletly BCom MA & Nicholas Ritchie MA(Oxon)
Second edition

A readable account of deregulation and the financial revolution in the City of London in the late 1980s, by two economics masters at Eton College, updated after the stockmarket crash of October 1987. 'A timely study...reveals all.' *Times Educational Supplement*. 'Forthright and opinionated.' *Financial Decisions*. 'The most easily accessible...each of its chapters is short, digestible and covers a lot of ground.' *The Financial Times*.

Paperback, 122 pages, illustrated.

The Crash and the Coming Crisis
Guy Galletly BCom MA

The record collapse of world stockmarkets in 1987 sent shockwaves throughout the international financial system. Did it mark the beginning of a long and ominous new downwave in the global economy? What does it mean for the individual citizen and investor? Written by a young economics master at Eton College, the book offers a fascinating case study of financial markets in turmoil. Complete with charts.

Paperback, 128 pages, illustrated.

The Business of Banking
Don Wright & Wally Valentine
Second edition

An officially recommended textbook for students taking the Preliminary Certificate course of the Chartered Institute of Bankers, coauthored by the Chief Examiner of the 'Business of Banking' paper. The book provides an ideal introduction for everyone wanting a clear understanding of how Britain's financial services industry functions today. 'Heads the reading list for the Banking Certificate's Business of Banking paper.' *Banking World*. 'A lively and appropriate text.... This volume can be highly recommended, not only for the clarity of its text and wealth of illustration, but also because of the authority of its authors.' *Association of Banking Teachers Bulletin*.

Paperback, 256 pages, illustrated.

An Introduction to Bank Lending
Peter Anderson ACIOB

Today's professional lender must not only be able to understand complex business accounts; he (or she) must appreciate less tangible but equally important aspects of a business—its products and markets, and the nature of its entrepreneur. How important *are* financial ratios? What security should a lender take for different forms of borrowing? How far should a lender trust to instinct? Written for young professional bankers and banking students, this lively and informative book meets the need for a clear introduction to how banks lend today.

Paperback, 160 pages, illustrated.

How to Buy & Run a Shop
Iain Maitland

The retail sector is notorious for the number of small shops which fail in their first few years. This step-by-step guide offers a positive method of running a retail shop, how and where to trade, getting finance, promotion, trouble-shooting, records and accounts, employment and consumer law, tricks of the trade, and is complete with case studies and references. 'With its clear step-by-step approach it sets out all you need to know.' *Independent Retailer*.

Paperback, 176 pages, illustrated. HOW TO Books.

How to Start a Business from Home
Graham Jones BSc

Explains everything you need to start a successful home-based business, and capitalise on your interests, skills and experience, with all the secrets of how to turn a home into an office and spare time into cash. Complete with a wealth of ideas, suggested projects and checklists. An ideal companion for every business start-up. 'Full of ideas and advice.' *The Daily Mirror*.

Paperback, 160 pages, illustrated. HOW TO Books.

101 Great Money-Making Ideas
Mark Hempshell

An essential handbook for everyone seeking extra cash to spend, a profitable new business idea to develop, or complete financial independence: packed with proven cash-raising projects to suit every interest and age group. Mark Hempshell is a young entrepreneur who has successfully developed a network of new businesses.

Paperback and hardback, 239 pages, illustrated.

How to Keep Business Accounts
Peter Taylor FCA FCCA

An easy-to-understand handbook for everyone new to this import-ant subject, showing how to set up and run a double-entry book-keeping system. 'A compact and direct introduction.' *Journal of the Society of Association Executives*. 'A useful handbook for owners, managers and students alike.' *Mind Your Own Business Magazine*.

Paperback, 176 pages, illustrated. HOW TO Books.

How to Raise Business Finance
Peter Ibbetson ACIOB

Written by a professional banker this book meets the need for a step-by-step handbook for every business owner and manager needing finance for start up, for cash flow, research and develop-ment, new equipment, premises or export. 'Gives the right amount of information.' *Association of British Chambers of Commerce*. 'A lucid account of the steps by which a small businessman can substantially strengthen his case.' *The Financial Times*.

Paperback, 160 pages, illustrated. HOW TO Books.